DRUGS

Anita Naik

Illustrated by Sarah Nayler

h
Hodder
Children's

To My Parents

*With thanks to the readers of Just 17 Magazine
and to the Durham and Darlington Drug Action Team*

Text copyright 1997 © Anita Naik
Illustrations copyright 1997 © Sarah Nayler
Cover photograph courtesy of the Robert Harding Picture Library
Published by Hodder Children's Books 1997

Consultant: David Cliff, Drugs Action Co-ordinator,
Durham and Darlington Drug Action Team
Design by Fiona Webb

10 9 8 7 6 5 4 3

ISBN: 0 340 69973 6

Printed by Guernsey Press Ltd, Guernsey, Channel Islands.

Hodder Children's Books
a division of Hodder Headline Limited
338 Euston Road
London NW1 3BH

Introduction

When I was 11 years old I was certain that I was anti-drugs and convinced they only led to one thing – death. I didn't know anyone who took drugs and imagined a typical drug-user as some low-life who didn't know any better. In my mind the drugs issue was pretty simple – you just said no and walked away. Then I started secondary school and most of my so-called drug-free friends started smoking and drinking. Soon I too was tempted. Not only because it looked cool, but because I knew not doing these things would mean being left out in the cold. By the time I got to college, some of my friends were experimenting heavily with drugs. It was then that I realised people who take drugs are ordinary people like you and me. Looking back now, most of these friends admit they had no idea what they were getting into. They vaguely knew the health risks, but, like everyone else, thought it would never happen to them. Most wish someone had warned them of the long-term dangers – but this wasn't considered part of drugs education at the time. Nowadays, experts believe that educating yourself about the harmful side-effects of drug-taking will help you make a fully-informed choice about what's right for you. This book isn't here to tell you what to do or what not to do. It will simply tell you what happens when someone does take drugs. After all, we are all responsible for ourselves and we all have to make our own choices. This book will help you find out all you need to know to do just that.

Anita

Contents

CHAPTER ONE

What are drugs?

"Drugs are things that can kill you." Toby (12)

"Drugs are illegal pills and stuff." Sian (13)

"Drugs are like medicines that people use for other things, like going out." Lisa (13)

"Ecstasy, dope, heroin – they're all drugs." Tina (14)

"Real drugs are Ecstasy and Crack, other drugs are aspirin and things." Tom (13)

What kind of things come into your head when someone says the word 'drugs' to you? Do you immediately think of Ecstasy and Heroin? Or does your local chemist and the hospital come to mind? Maybe you consider alcohol and cigarettes as drugs – or perhaps you think only illegal substances are 'real' drugs.

According to the Oxford English Dictionary, a drug is a medicinal substance – however that's a rather imprecise definition. It would be fairer to say that a drug is a chemical substance which alters the mood of your body i.e. the way you feel, the way you think, the way you experience and the way you behave.

WHAT ARE LEGAL DRUGS?

These are things which you may not usually think of as drugs, such as aspirin, coffee, sugar – even tea. Coffee and tea contain caffeine, which is a stimulant. This means it makes you feel very awake. Another example is sugar, which affects your body's insulin (blood energy levels), making you feel high or low. Apart from these readily–available drugs, there are a whole variety of drugs you may have been prescribed when you were ill – cough mixtures, cold remedies or headache tablets, for example. These are more powerful drugs which can harm you if not taken correctly. This is why they have to be bought from pharmacies or prescribed by a doctor, so you can be advised on the correct dose.

These drugs are classed as legal because, if used according to the directions on the packet or in moderation, they won't cause you to become ill or give you serious side effects, and are usually safely manufactured in legitimately licenced labs.

Of course, cigarettes, alcohol and solvents are the exceptions here. These *are* dangerous and *can* kill you but are still legal (see chapters on Smoking, Alcohol and Solvents).

WHAT ARE ILLEGAL DRUGS?

Drugs which fall under this category are the drugs which you read about in the papers: Ecstasy, Cannabis, LSD, Heroin, Speed, Cocaine and Crack. With these drugs there is a risk of becoming so hooked that users don't want to live without them. Most of these drugs can kill and all of them have dangerous side-effects.

THE LANGUAGE OF DRUGS

As you can see, the whole arena of drugs and what is and isn't good for you is very confusing. What's more, it's so rife with myths that sometimes the truth gets lost. In order to understand this whole subject and get to grips with what each of these drugs can do to your body,

Ugh!

-er

LANGUAGE OF DRUGS

you first need to get your head around some practical terms:

• **Addiction** – This is when a drug is craved so much that it is impossible to stop taking it. Usually an addiction is present when the drug has altered the chemical balance of the body, which in turn affects the body's natural processes.

• **Tolerance** – This is when the body gets so used to a drug that larger and larger amounts of the drug are needed in order to maintain the same feeling.

• **Psychological dependence** – This is when someone needs to keep taking a drug to feel okay and cope with their life. They feel they can't cope without drugs, even though their body is not physically dependent. Despite the popular view that it's only drugs that create a psychological dependency, you can actually become dependent on just about anything – whether it's a boyfriend or girlfriend, gambling or chocolate.

• **Physical dependence** – This is when drugs have been taken on such a regular basis that the body needs regular doses to avoid withdrawal symptoms.

• **Hard drugs** – This is a term used to describe drugs which have powerful effects, such as Heroin and Cocaine. These drugs are addictive and hard to give up.

• **Soft drugs** – These are drugs which are taken for social purposes (also known as Recreational Drugs) i.e. Cannabis. They do not have withdrawal symptoms when given up. However, soft drugs are not safe. They have long–term side–effects and can be addictive.

- **Drug misuse** – This is a fairly broad term which can be used in two ways – either to describe drugs which are not illegal but are being used in the wrong way, as with glue sniffing or overuse of prescription drugs, or as a way to refer to all illegal drug use.

- **Drug abuse** – Used to describe a person who is using drugs (normally illegal drugs) in a harmful way.

- **User** – Someone who takes drugs.

- **Dealer** – Or Pusher. Someone who sells drugs.

- **Withdrawal symptoms** – Physical and mental reactions to a drug being denied to a user, for example, shaking, sweating, vomiting, night terrors and anxiety attacks.

- **Depressants** – These slow down the activity of the brain, creating a feeling of relaxation, sleepiness and a loss of anxiety, e.g. Heroin.

- **Stimulants** – These increase the activity of the brain and make people feel more alert, energetic and awake, e.g. Caffeine, Speed, Ecstasy.

- **Hallucinogenic** – These are drugs which distort the senses. They can cause users to see and hear things that are not really there, e.g. LSD.

- **High** – A word used to describe the good feeling users have under the influence of drugs.

- **Gateway drugs** – Drugs which are thought to lead to the use of more dangerous drugs. For instance, lots of people believe smoking cannabis encourages users to go on to try harder drugs. This has never been proven to be true. However, there *is* evidence to suggest that alcohol and cigarettes may be 'gateway' drugs.

A BRIEF HISTORY OF DRUGS

The use and abuse of drugs is so old, it's practically impossible to find a date for its beginning. Many ancient cultures are known to have used drugs for religious purposes: to invoke trances, to aid meditation, or for ritualistic reasons. Even now, some Native American tribes use the powerful hallucinogenic drug Peyote in their religious ceremonies.

Other drugs have been used for centuries for medicinal reasons, as in South America, where the native people chew the leaves of the Coca plant to deal with fatigue. It's a perfectly acceptable drug to them, and yet Cocaine, derived from the same leaves, is illegal here. The classification of different drugs as legal or illegal has varied over the centuries – in the 1700s there was an attempt to make coffee an illegal substance in England, while in America alcohol was actually banned for a time under the 1920s Prohibition laws. Many of the drugs which are now banned in the UK, such as Opium, MDMA (Ecstasy), Cannabis and LSD, have a legal medicinal past.

While some countries or individuals may think one type of drug is OK, they may clamp down or avoid others. A parent who smokes 40 cigarettes a day may lecture you on drinking without seeing any problem. The government may continute to campaign against drugs whilst profiting from the sale of cigarettes and alcohol in the form of taxation. Wherever you go and whatever you read, it's likely that you'll always find discrepancies and hypocrisy where drugs are concerned. This is why your best bet is to make up your own mind. Learn all you can and then make an informed decision about whether or not drugs are for you.

WHY DO PEOPLE TAKE DRUGS?

"I take them for pleasure." Tim (12)

"I take them because I want to." Lyn (15)

"I haven't taken drugs yet, but I'll probably try them. I don't want to get hooked, I just want to see what they're like." Kelly (13)

"I've heard you get the most amazing visions and feel totally cool about everything." Jez (14)

"I don't take drugs but I think people do because they feel everyone's doing it, so they should too." Amanda (14)

If you listen to what the papers say, you may think that young people take drugs because they're forced into it by evil dealers or because they're bored and fed up and can't think of anything better to do. While some people may drink or take drugs out of boredom, the fact is that all kinds of people have all kinds of different reasons.

- Some do it because the thought of missing out on an 'amazing' experience is just too much for them.
- Others try it because they feel bad about themselves and hope a drug will make them feel better.
- Some people just do it to escape from their lives, others to fit in with their friends.

There isn't any one reason why people take drugs. If you asked a cross–section of people who took drugs why they did it, you'd probably find a whole variety of reasons, some thought–provoking, others just plain ridiculous.

The fact is, not many people manage to get through life without ever once using drugs, whether illegal or legal, so you need to be informed enough to know what you're doing.

REASONS WHY PEOPLE TAKE DRUGS

For fun

"People always go on about the dangers of drugs and why kids take them. They say it's because we're unhappy, or miserable, or lonely. Well, I can tell them why we do it, we do it for fun!"

Jacqui (15)

As Jacqui points out, drugs are tempting for a number of reasons, but the one reason that often gets ignored is pleasure. It's this desire for fun and excitement that makes many people forget the danger element of drugs.

Peer pressure

"I do it because my friends do. They don't force me to smoke, I just do it because I want to show them I'm in with them. I don't think they'd ditch me if I gave up but I don't know."

Tim (15)

Apart from believing that it's fun to get 'out of your head' many people find it pretty hard to say no to drugs when everyone else is doing it, or at least talking about it.

Curiosity

"You hear so much about drugs that it makes you want to try them. Even the down things make it sound quite exciting."

Lee (13)

Everyone wants to try out new experiences, and this desire to see what drugs are like makes many people experiment with them, often without realising what the 'down' side really entails.

Accessibility

"Drugs are everywhere. My mum thinks you can only get them at clubs but there's a guy down the road who sells stuff and some boys who hang out near our school."

Will (14)

It's a myth that drugs are expensive and hard to find. Most drugs like LSD, solvents and cannabis, are cheaper than alcohol and just as easy to get hold of, which makes them more of a temptation.

Feeling Grown Up

"I smoke because it makes me feel older and mature. I also like the look of smoking – it's cool and sexy. I know about the health risks but they don't bother me because they only happen to you when you're old, not when you're 14."

Seema (14)

I smoked because it made me look older... now I do

Deciding to take drugs is a risk and therefore makes some users feel grown up and mature. Girls like Seema consider themselves in control of their own lives by the fact they can choose to do something dangerous.

Rebellion

> "My mum is always nagging on about the dangers of drugs. She harps on and on about how people who take E are a danger to society and should be locked up. The joke is, I take E and she doesn't even know it. That kills me every time I think of it."

Erica (14)

Some people use drugs as a way of getting back at their parents, guardians or teachers. It's a way of saying, 'You can't tell me what to do with my body'.

For confidence

> "I drink for courage. When I'm at a party and sober I feel shy, unconfident and miserable. When I'm drunk everyone loves me. I'm happy, together and good fun. That's why I drink – so people like me."

Tina (14)

Lots of people use drugs in the hope they will make them feel better about themselves. It's a way of covering up problems and avoiding real issues that need to be tackled.

To cope with exam pressure

> "I can never cope when exams come round. I never seem to have enough time to do stuff so I end up having to stay up all night. A little while ago my friend gave me these pills to help me stay awake. They make me cranky and achy but they really help me to stay awake and concentrate."

Ben (16)

Work pressure is a very common reason why people start taking drugs. They use them to cope with stress and anxiety and often don't realise they are only adding to their problems.

To cope with being bullied and abused

"I hate my new school. My mum really wants me to like it here, so I can't let her down and tell her how everyone hates me and calls me names. The only way I get through it all is to have a drink. My brother has always said alcohol is great for courage, so I try to make sure I have a drink before I walk through the school gates every morning. No-one suspects anything because he buys it for me and it looks like plain lemonade."

Shola (13)

Some people take drugs or abuse alcohol because they can't handle something bad that's happening to them. If you are being bullied, like Shola, or being physically or sexually abused, drugs aren't the solution to your problem. Telling someone is the only way to solve what's happening to you. Don't worry about what people will say about the drugs, concentrate first on protecting yourself by talking through what is happening with someone you trust. If a family member or relative is out of the question, contact Childline on 0800 1111.

To improve body image

"I'm tempted to take steroids because I want a good body like the ones you see down at the gym. My friends tell me taking them gives you confidence without having to try too

hard. People talk about the side-effects, but I reckon it's
worth it."

Nick (14)

Anabolic steroids do build up muscle and strength in
the first instance, but in the long-term, they
significantly reduce life expectation through damage
to the heart and liver as well as carrying other health
risks.

"My friend told me that speed can help you to lose
weight. I hate the way I look and took up smoking when
I was 12 because I heard it made you lose weight – it
didn't. But speed does. I've lost loads."

Vanessa (16)

In the 1960s, Amphetamine (Speed) was commonly
prescribed as a slimming aid because of its appetite
suppressant qualities. These days Amphetamines are
very rarely prescribed, because of the health risks.
Minimal use does get rid of hunger pangs, but only
until the drug wears off, when users are likely to feel
ravenously hungry and totally exhausted.

WHAT KIND OF PEOPLE ARE DRUG-USERS?

"I used to think drug-users were the creepy people at
school, you know, the ones who didn't say anything and
hung out by the gates – now I know a drug-user can be
anyone, anyone at all."

Paul (14)

"My friends all take Ecstasy. They are not ravers or mad like the people you see in the papers. They're just like me. I haven't done it because I worry about the down side but I know one day I'll try it."

Sue (14)

The popular image of a drug-user is either a skinny down–and–out addicted to heroin, living in a squat and begging on the street, or a mad raver off his head on Ecstasy, dancing the night away and heading for disaster. If that's how you think of drug-users I can hardly blame you. Thanks to the media, the image of drug-users has been wildly exaggerated. In actual fact there is no stereotypical drug-user. Descriptions like the ones above are pathetic because they make everyone think you can spot someone with a drug problem a mile off, when the truth is you can't.

"I had a very clear image of who a drug-user was – and it wasn't me. I was clean-cut, didn't go to raves and didn't drink, therefore in my mind I didn't have a problem. I knew I wouldn't be caught dead out of my head on the street and I knew I was never going to get arrested. Yet, every weekend when my parents went away, me and my friends would take Ecstasy, Speed or whatever we could get our hands on."

Stephen (17)

"My friends and I took drugs for years. Usually in our bedroom at sleepovers or at lunchtime at school. But I would never have called us your typical drug-users. Thinking about it now, we probably were."

Anna (16)

Which one is the addict?

MYTHS ABOUT PEOPLE WHO USE DRUGS

• **They are losers** – Society is very judgmental about people who take drugs. The media in particular are very unforgiving and this is why some people consider people with drug problems to be losers. The fact is, they aren't, they just have a problem and need help, not labels.

• **Most will die** – Thankfully the majority of people who use illegal drugs *don't* die. This is because most people just dabble out of curiosity and very few become addicted. To put things in perspective – illegal drugs kill about 300 people a year in Britain, while alcohol kills nearly 30,000 a year and smoking results in over 100,000 premature deaths. This *doesn't* mean drugs are safe – they're not. Whatever you take there will be a range of health risks, from short–term side–effects to long–term problems (see specific chapters for details). If in doubt, don't do it!

• **They're from deprived backgrounds** – Another big myth is that drug abuse is rife only in poor areas. But statistics show that drug abuse happens everywhere, so don't be fooled.

• **There's something wrong with them** – *"Sane people don't take drugs"* – this is a quote from a teacher I used to have. People who take drugs aren't mad (even if you think they're crazy to try them), it's more likely they try them for a variety of reasons – from experimentation to curiosity.

• **They're all addicts** – It takes time to become addicted to a certain drug. Contrary to what people might say, you can't just take a drug once and become addicted. However, there *are* some drugs, like Heroin and Crack Cocaine, that are very easy to become quickly addicted to.

• **They have addictive personalities** – These days everyone thinks they're a psychologist and this is how terms like the one above get misused. There is no such thing as one type of personality being more prone to drug-taking than another. However, there *are* people who have problems that are more likely to lead them into an addiction.

MORE DRUG MYTHS

Saying no to drugs is easy

Some people are sure they will never take illicit drugs or other potentially harmful substances and never do. Others believe they can say no to drugs but when the time comes, they find it's not so easy. It's great to be confident when it comes to drugs, but over confidence can lead to trouble. It can make you think you know it all and are safe when you might not be. Likewise, being a know–all about why people take drugs will also win you no friends. Contrary to popular belief there isn't a 'type' of person who takes drugs and becomes addicted.

It won't happen to me

Most people who take drugs do it for pleasure. They do it because they've heard how great it is and how amazing an experience it can be. No–one who takes drugs ever thinks they're going to end up dead or in hospital. Most of us in every day life go around thinking we're invincible and drug-users are no different. Be realistic, if you're going to do drugs, know the dangers before you do it. No–one who takes drugs is safe, no matter how careful they are. Remember, everyone thinks it won't happen to them, but it can and it does.

Drug addicts are always locked-up

There are a number of ways to treat drug addicts and locking them up in prison or in hospital isn't an option. Most big towns and cities have a local drug service, which aims to educate the local community and help anyone who needs more information or support in coming off drugs. This is usually done in collaboration with local GPs and hospitals. For people with more serious problems there are a number of rehab centres around the country where you can go for several weeks. Here, people who are heavily addicted can be gradually helped off a drug with the help of trained professionals. Unfortunately, many of these are private or have limited spaces, which is why most addicts are now helped on a day basis at local centres.

Drugs are just a youth problem

If you read the papers, listen to MPs and watch TV, you're likely to think drugs are just a youth problem. The popular idea of a drug-user is a young person who has no idea about what they're getting into. Don't be fooled by this. Drugs affect everyone. Addicts come from all backgrounds and all ages and live all kinds of lives.

No-one will help

Drugs are still a taboo subject for many people. Like sex, some people believe just talking about it promotes the idea that it's okay to do it. Other people make you feel guilty for asking questions because they believe it's a sign you obviously want to try them.

These common and ignorant notions can stop you from educating yourself about the dangers of drugs. Never be fooled into thinking no–one will talk to you about drugs. There are always informed people you can talk to about the facts. Other people who can help, but who you might not normally think of approaching are:

- A parent
- A friend's parent
- A teacher you trust
- Your GP (he or she will keep everything confidential)
- An older sister or brother
- A nurse at your local surgery
- A pharmacist at your local chemist
- Your local library
- Your school library
- Magazines

DRUGS AND THE LAW

Most people who use drugs think they'll never be caught. They also think that even if they *are* caught the police will let them off: after all, who cares about one tab of Ecstasy when there are big dealers out there? The truth is, the majority of people who are arrested for drugs are usually caught for something small. The law takes a dim view of people caught holding drugs (possession) and a worse view of those caught giving or selling them to their friends (supplying). If you are prosecuted, it will be under the Misuse of Drugs Act 1971, and you will be charged according to the type of drug you are found with, e.g. Class A, B or C. Drugs are categorised according to how dangerous they are, and the higher the class, the bigger the penalty if you get caught with them.

CLASS A drugs are Heroin, Cocaine, LSD, Ecstasy.
For possession – Up to 7 years in prison and a fine.
For supply – Life imprisonment and a fine.

CLASS B drugs are Cannabis, Amphetamines.
For possession – Up to 5 years in prison and a fine.
For supply – Up to 14 years in prison and a fine.

CLASS C drugs are tranquillisers, e.g. Valium (these are not illegal if they are prescribed for you – they *are* illegal if they are not.).
For possession – Up to 2 years in prison and a fine.
For supply – Up to 5 years in prison and a fine.

Anyone possessing, growing, importing, exporting or supplying drugs is breaking the law. Don't be fooled into thinking your age will act as an excuse. It won't. If you are aged between 10 and 14, you are still classified as a child, but can be convicted of a criminal offence if the prosecution can prove you knew what you were doing was wrong. Once you are over 14, you are still classified as a young person and tried in a youth court, but will have full criminal responsibility for your actions, in the same way as an adult. If you are caught with drugs and prosecuted, the following can happen:

Under 14 – Depending on the type and the amount of the drug you are caught with, you may receive a caution for your first offence, and your parents will be informed. For a second offence, you are likely to have to appear in a youth court and, if sentenced, may have restrictions placed on where you live, what you're allowed to do and what school you can go to. It may also involve counselling. You will normally have to have your parents present and they may be made responsible for your acts.

Over 14 – As above, unless you are linked with an adult offender, in which case you will have to attend a magistrates court rather than a youth court, and a custodial sentence or fine may be a possibility, depending on the severity of the offence.

THE LAW AND ALCOHOL

You cannot buy alcohol until you are 18. You can be fined up to £1000 for trying to buy or drink alcohol on licensed premises. Your parents are also committing a criminal offence if they give you alcohol under the age of five. If they buy you a drink in a bar when you are under 18, or send you to buy alcohol for them from an off–licence or supermarket they can be prosecuted, as can the shopkeepers who sell it to you.

THE LAW AND SMOKING

It is an offence for a shopkeeper to sell cigarettes (also cigars, loose tobacco or cigarette papers) to a person under 16, whether or not it is for their own use. While it is not an offence for an under 16 year old to smoke or be in possession of cigarettes, if they are caught smoking in public, they may legally have their cigarettes confiscated by a police officer.

CHAPTER TWO

Drugs and peer pressure

ARE YOU UNDER PRESSURE?

1 Your friends all smoke. How do you feel?
   a) Curious – you wouldn't mind seeing what all the fuss is about.
   b) Anxious – you know they all want you to smoke too.
   c) Irritated – it's a dirty, smelly habit and everyone knows it causes cancer.

2 You fancy a boy who is known for getting drunk all the time. You want him to like you, what do you do?
   a) Start getting drunk when you're around him so he knows you're game for a laugh.

b) Tell him about how bad alcohol is for him and hope he'll see how much you care.

c) Drink the same brand of beer as him and hope he notices.

3 **Your sister says she's found a great diet. It consists of smoking and drinking coffee. What do you do?**

a) Talk to your sister and encourage her to be more healthy.

b) Give it a try, you wouldn't mind losing a couple of pounds.

c) Feel worried about her but try the diet anyway.

4 **You're at a party and all your mates are smoking cannabis. What do you do?**

a) Ignore them – if they want to be stupid it's up to them.

b) Ignore them – but feel left out and a bit tempted.

c) Join in – what's the harm?

5 **How often do you pay attention to anti-drink and drug adverts?**

a) Never

b) Sometimes

c) All the time

SCORES

1	A	5	B	10	C	0
2	A	10	B	0	C	5
3	A	0	B	5	C	10
4	A	0	B	5	C	10
5	A	10	B	5	C	0

RESULTS

0 – 15

You know what's what when it comes to drugs. You're also in the minority and aren't tempted or even a bit curious about trying stuff out. Good for you, but remember not to be too judgmental about people who give in to pressure or choose to experiment. Giving them a hard time won't make them stop, it will just make them stop listening to you.

20 – 35

Phew! Are you under pressure or what? On the one hand you're worried about drugs and on the other you're afraid of being left out by everyone. You know about the downside of drugs, so you have to make a decision that's right for you. But remember this – anyone who throws away your friendship just because you won't try drugs out isn't worth worrying about.

40 – 50

You could do with learning a bit more about drugs – and that includes smoking and alcohol. It's all very well being curious but throwing yourself into drugs just to get attention, or for excitement, is bad news. Do yourself a favour – educate yourself before you hurt yourself.

Your peers are the people you hang around with, normally the same age as yourself. Peer pressure means your friends and schoolmates pressurising you to do things you don't really want to get involved in. Sometimes it's easier to go with the crowd – after all, you want your friends to like you and you don't want to be left out. If all your friends drink, smoke or dabble with drugs, it can be difficult to resist joining in – even when you know about the health risks and the fact that they are breaking the law. In an ideal world, you could hold your head up and say NO to everything offered to you without feeling left out, boring or square. Sadly, this isn't an ideal world and often saying yes is a lot easier than saying no.

"It's not as simple as saying no and still being friends. Even if they're okay with that, it's still horrible to be the odd one out. It's like they all belong to a club and you don't, so you don't know what they're talking about."

Karen (14)

a pint ... of Orange juice please

Being friends is pretty complicated at any age. The fact is, despite what your parents think, friends seem everything during your school years. The more you belong to a group of friends the easier your life seems to be, which is why it's hard to make a decision that risks their rejection. It's okay for adults to tell you to stick up for yourself but how can you, when that means being made to feel uncomfortable and uncool?

"Most of my friends smoke and I don't. My best friend recently told me that everyone thought I was too scared to smoke and that I was being a baby about it. This really upsets me. What if that got round – no boy would want to come near me."

Sue (13)

SIGNS THAT YOU'RE UNDER PRESSURE

- Friends make fun of you for not smoking or drinking.
- You start being left out of things just because you refuse to smoke, drink or take drugs.

- People accuse you of saying no because you're scared.
- Friends act as if they're older and wiser than you just because they do drugs.
- You're told that the opposite sex find smoking and drinking sexy.
- You start smoking and drinking to please your friends.
- You feel people won't like you if you say no.

THE STRANGE THING ABOUT PEER PRESSURE

"My friends all smoke dope. I don't but it's hard. They act like I'm too childish to understand how good it is and are always trying to persuade me to take a toke (a puff). I still say no, but I always end up sitting there feeling like I'm the odd one out."

Sam (14)

"Everyone drinks, so it's hard not to. I don't even like the taste but I'll still stand there with a glass of something. It's too awkward not to."

Donna (14)

Oh Lovely

Gulp...

"Sometimes when mum goes to work, my older brother Steve and I sneak mouthfuls of alcohol from her drinks cupboard. I was quite afraid the first time but Steve said he did it all the time. Last summer holidays we managed to get through a whole bottle of wine and one of gin and mum never even noticed."

Tom (11)

The odd thing about peer pressure is that sometimes you may not even realise it's happening to you. Maybe your friends say it's okay for you to say no to drugs and then act as if it isn't.

"When I told my friends there was no way I was going to start smoking, they said that it was okay and up to me. But since then they've started to go off without me, usually to the park. I asked them why, and they said I'd hate it because I'd be out of it as everyone down there smokes."

Lucy (13)

Maybe you feel you should try drugs so your friends will stop treating you as though you're boring or square.

"I've never taken drugs ever, but when I'm with my friends I pretend I've taken E. They all reckon they have and I know what they think of people who don't take drugs. It's a stupid lie, I know it is, and I know one day they're going to expect me to take a tab with them. That's quite a frightening thought because I know I'll have to do it."

Mandy (14)

Perhaps you're tempted to give in to peer pressure so you're no longer the odd one out.

> "I hate drinking, it tastes disgusting but I keep doing it because everyone does. None of my friends force me to drink and I don't make them do it. Sometimes I think I'll give up but when we're out and hanging about, someone always has drink on them and so I feel I have to do it."
>
> Mark (14)

On the other hand, maybe you think experimenting with drugs might make you stand out in your crowd, get attention or be the leader. Maybe you associate drug-taking with maturity. Perhaps you think it will eliminate your shyness and make you feel confident.

The real problem is, of course, that drink and drugs aren't a solution to any of these problems. They *won't* make you more confident, in fact, they'll have the opposite effect. They'll make you feel that you aren't anything without them and that they are the only way you'll get through life.

As for peer pressure, taking drugs doesn't prove you're a good friend. And it doesn't prove your friends are mature, cool or trendy. Real friends don't encourage you to do dangerous things, even if they're into them. Remember, someone who is cool with what they are doing doesn't need to get a band of followers to back them up. Often people put pressure on you to do stuff with them because they're scared of doing it alone.

MYTHS ABOUT PEER PRESSURE AND DRUGS

Only other people get hooked or hurt by drugs

"I feel sorry for the people who die but that's usually because they've taken too much. Me and my friends are careful. We never take too much."

Paul (14)

Part of the problem with drugs is that most users think they're invincible. They believe that the dangers will never affect them because it's other people who end up being rushed to hospital, other people who can't handle the effects of drugs.

If you're someone who is tempted to take drugs or are even taking drugs right now – whether it be alcohol, cigarettes or Ecstasy – don't ignore the information and warnings. Drugs can and do kill. They don't discriminate – it could happen to anyone.

People get their drugs from pushers

"We don't get our E from some bloke we don't even know. We buy it off this guy in the sixth form, he gets it from his brother. This way we know it's safe and not the rubbish you hear about in the paper."

Liz (15)

"My mum thinks it was my school mates who got me into smoking but it wasn't. It was my sister. I caught her smoking once and she offered me a few cigarettes if I promised to keep quiet about it."

Damon (14)

Contrary to popular belief, most people come into contact with drugs through friends and older sisters and brothers, not through anonymous pushers on the street. What's more, being approached by someone you like makes saying no harder and more complicated.

"I really admire Tara. She's pretty, fun and always looks great. When she first started talking to me I was really happy because I'm not usually friends with people like her. I already knew she smoked and drank, and I wasn't surprised, but when she offered me a cigarette, I was too afraid to say no. I know it's stupid but I want her to like me and think I'm mature too."

Fran (13)

Of course, if a friend was direct about his or her tactics, e.g. If you don't smoke I won't like you – most people would have no problem with saying no. Unfortunately, peer pressure doesn't happen like this. Often people put *themselves* under pressure, imagining that they won't be liked, loved or accepted if they refuse to do what their friends are doing.

All drugs are dangerous

"I'm always hearing all drugs are dangerous and can kill you. I think that's a load of rubbish. I smoke quite a lot of dope and it's never done anything bad to me. It makes me think the rest of the things you hear are a load of rubbish and not true."

Maz (14)

The danger when taking drugs depends on many things, such as *what* you've taken, *how much* you've taken, and your state of mind at the time. Although some drugs are less dangerous than others, illegally–manufactured drugs are *always* a danger because it's impossible to tell what's in them. Also, as size and thickness differ all the time, never trust a friend who tells you something's safe because they've tried it. Everyone reacts differently to drugs – body size, weight, age and sex all need to be taken into account. Remember, if a drug is stronger than you think and you don't know what's in it, it's more likely to hurt you.

Soft drugs lead to hard drugs

> "I've heard that smoking cannabis often leads people to smoke crack. That's what worries me, my boyfriend smokes all the time, does this mean he'll be an addict?"
>
> Mel (14)

One of the greatest myths of all time is that taking soft drugs automatically means you'll end up on hard drugs. There is no evidence to suggest that this is true, though drinking heavily does increase your chances of trying other drugs. Also, taking any kind of drug does increase your chances of coming into contact with 'harder drugs'. This is because drugs like Ecstasy, Speed and LSD are often mixed with other substances, and are often available through the same sources. What you have to remember with drugs is that you always have a choice. A choice not to take them, a choice to stop taking them and a choice not to go any further.

Drugs are cool

> "My sister's friend used to be a model and she said the girls were all skinny because they smoked all the time and took drugs. She said it wasn't like they were addicts or anything, it was just what people do when they're well-known."
>
> Tammy (13)

Sadly, drugs have got a pretty cool image because pop stars, models, actors, actresses and other famous people are often associated with them. How many times do you see a picture of some famous person with a drink in their hand or a cigarette hanging out of their mouth? By association, drinking and smoking begin to look cool. But the other side of the story is more tragic. People in these professions (and in other not so glamorous jobs) often end up taking drugs to deal with their high–pressure lifestyle and then find they can't get by without them. Many end up in drug clinics, alcohol rehab units or even dead. What's cool about that?

HOW TO TURN DOWN DRUGS AND STILL STAY FRIENDS

Sometimes saying no just doesn't work. Friends still try to persuade you you're wrong and that you should give drugs a try. It's tough, but you can get round this by not letting yourself be swayed.

I could give you a list of lines to say to help you turn down drugs but, let's face it, you have to say no in your own way or it won't work. This way you'll feel more strongly about what you're saying, and will get your point across in the most confident way possible.

However, remembering the following will help:
- No–one can make you feel inferior without your consent. Being trendy, cool and mature are all things that come from the inside of ourselves and have nothing to do with what we drink, smoke or swallow.
- Say no and don't feel bad about it. Obsessing about what you've said, how you've said it, and what people think of you is bad news.

- Being the only non drug-taker may feel awkward and uncomfortable but this just a phase and, like all awkward phases, it will pass.
- Don't make things worse for yourself by letting your imagination exaggerate a situation. Being the odd one out is hard but it doesn't mean your friends no longer like you.

"When I refused to smoke drugs at a party, I thought all my friends thought I was being stupid. I got so upset about it that I went home early and cried. Over the weekend I decided that if they didn't like me for not taking drugs, I wasn't going to be friends with them any more. When I got to school on Monday, I was all ready to fight with them but then I found out they were all worried about me and had no idea why I'd got so upset."

Tina (14)

- Strange but true, no–one is judging you. Everyone is so worried about themselves and how they look to other people that they aren't even thinking about you.

- Question people who try to bully you into taking drugs. After all, if drugs are so brilliant, why is it so necessary for them to have your company? If some one is giving you grief for saying no, ask them the following:
  - Why is it so important for you to take them?
  - Why are they so stressed out about you saying no?
  - Why do they have to make other people take them too?

COPING WITH FRIENDS WHO DRINK/ TAKE DRUGS

How To Spot Someone With a Drug Problem

- Erratic mood swings, may be aggressive and/or lethargic.
- Loss of appetite – no interest in food at all.
- Depression and anxiety – paranoia or unhappiness that won't lift.
- Need for more money than usual – possibly increased borrowing or stealing.
- Strange sores on the body or marks on arms (only in some cases).
- Unusual smells or stains on clothes.
- Inability to concentrate.
- Loss of interest in usual interests and hobbies.

The dilemma when dealing with a friend who has a serious drugs problem is basically, should you take responsibility for them or leave them to do what they want? Often people choose not to get involved, simply because they don't want the hassle, or else they imagine their friend will hate them for interfering. What you have to weigh up is how serious their problem is and what kind of help you think they need.

Ask yourself the following:

- Are they a danger to themselves?
- Are they a danger to others?
- How far has their life slipped because of drug-taking? Are they skipping school, not eating, not sleeping or stealing to afford their habit, for example?
- Does anyone else know what's going on?
- Do you suspect they're secretly crying out for help?
- Are they involved with people who are dangerous?

Answering these questions will help you to determine just how serious you think their problem may be.

There is no easy answer, but the bottom line is, how bad will you feel if something happens to your friend and you never did anything to help them? Telling doesn't mean you have to tell the police or the teachers in your school. It means finding someone you trust who will help. An older brother or sister, a relative, even a parent, can all help you to put a friend's problem in perspective and work out what kind of help (if any) they may need. Confidential helplines (see page 45) can also offer support, and information.

"I knew my sister had been taking drugs for about a year but I didn't feel I could say anything because she was older than me. One day I came home and my mum said she'd been rushed to hospital with a suspected overdose. I felt so guilty. I kept thinking if only I'd said something this wouldn't have happened."

Helen (12)

"I tried to help my friend a number of times. I tried to talk to him, got leaflets for him and offered to go to get help with him, but he refused everything. In the end I had to tell his mum. It still didn't help. He still takes loads of drugs and nothing anyone says seems to do anything. I used to feel bad about this – and guilty – but I don't any more. I tried and that's all I could do. It's not my fault he won't give up."

Will (16)

COPING WITH PARENTS WITH DRINK/ DRUGS PROBLEMS

"My dad drinks all the time. My mum says he hasn't got a problem, but she's fooling herself. He lost his job because of his drinking, he gets into fights all the time and sometimes he's so drunk he doesn't even come home. He's a joke."

Mike (12)

"My mum left my dad because of his drug problem. I don't know what drug, but once I saw him on the street and he looked disgusting. He hardly recognised me and tried to get me to give him some money."

Jules (16)

"My mum has a problem but everyone in my family pretends she doesn't. They say she's stressed and that's why she drinks. Or she's unhappy and needs to drink. It's rubbish – she's got a problem and needs help."

Tanya (14)

Sometimes families cover up secrets and problems because they can't face up to the reality of a situation. When this happens it can be hard to carry on with your own life. Maybe you feel you have to be the one who helps out, covers up or even lies about what's going on. Perhaps your parents even expect you to do this. If a parent's behaviour is affecting your life to the point where you're worried all the time, you need to do something. You might have to be the voice of reason, the one who says, What's going on here? Or the person who seeks outside help from an agency, a trusted friend or another adult.

Sometimes your parents' habits won't affect you directly and yet you still find yourself worried. It's at this point that you need to get your fears into perspective and talk to your parents. For instance, if your parents have one or two drinks when they come home from work, it doesn't automatically make them alcoholics. However, if your parents turn to drugs (drinking included) every time something goes wrong, become violent when they drink or put drink (for example) before everything else in their life then the chances are they have a problem and you need to seek help.

Remember, it's impossible to stop a drinker from drinking, it's only when they admit they have a problem and want to get better, that they'll stop. This means no amount of begging, crying or threatening is going to do any good to them or to you. This *doesn't* mean you should just ignore the fact that they drink. In fact, talking things through with them when they're sober may help you to understand them better. At the same time it may help them to see the pressure they're putting you under.

LOOKING AFTER YOURSELF

- Having a parent with an addiction is never your fault, even if they tell you it is. Whatever you do, don't blame yourself.
- Is your life or that of your brothers or sisters at risk? Are your parents a danger to themselves when they drink? Do you have to stay away from school in order to look after them? If the answer to any of these problems is yes, you need to seek help (see page 45).
- Asking for help won't get your parents into trouble, or mean you'll end up in care.
- Think about yourself. It's easy to forget what you're going through when you live with an addict of some sort. Recognise how you feel and talk to someone you trust.

COPING WITH PARENTS WHO ARE ANTI-EVERYTHING

"My parents are so anti-drugs, every time something comes on TV they rant about it. They say it's only ignorant kids who take E and stupid kids who get drunk. If they knew how my friends were, they'd go crazy and probably ban me from ever seeing them again. They are so old-fashioned, they don't realise everyone does drugs these days. Sometimes I just want to take something to shock them and make them see how wrong they are."

Tom (14)

Parents who are anti-everything are hard to deal with. More often than not it means they're not open to discussion and not open to hearing about what's really going on in your life. After all, who's going to be honest when they know it's going to be used against them? Try and recognise why your parents are behaving like this and you'll be more able to help ease their concerns.

1 Some parents act like a personal bodyguard because they're worried you're not going to make the right choice when it comes to drugs. The way to get them to stop policing you is to reassure them. Make it clear you're not going to be an idiot when it comes to drink and drugs. Don't come home drunk at midnight – and don't sneak about and not tell them where you're going. It's a pain having to be open about your life, but is being secretive about your whereabouts really worth all the hassle?

2 With the newspapers full of stories about young people dying from drugs and drink–related incidents, it's easy for parents to overreact and refuse to let you out of their sights. If this is happening to you, then a bit of careful negotiation is in order. Be open about who you're hanging out with, and make it clear you're not going to do something stupid. Don't miss your curfews, don't turn up drunk on the doorstep and don't frighten them with stories about how out of their head so and so got last night!

3 Some parents don't understand about drink and drugs simply because they've never come into contact with them. This makes them react very strongly to the whole subject. It may get on your nerves, but rubbishing their views, refusing to listen and storming out every time they have a rant won't get you anywhere. It will make them think you're about to do something dangerous and they'll be even tougher on you. Talking about drink and drugs sensibly is the only way you'll get them to see reason. Try approaching them with the right facts, get hold of some leaflets (see below), show them this book and reassure them that they can trust you.

HELP CONTACTS

ADFAM – the national charity for families and friends of drug users. They run a confidential helpline, providing information and support. 020 7928 8900.

NATIONAL DRUGS HELPLINE – 0800 776600

ALATEEN – Tel: 020 7403 0888 (alcohol)

CHILDLINE – 0800 1111

THE SAMARITANS – 0345 909090

RELEASE – 020 7603 8654 (help and advice for drugs users)

Don't forget you can also turn to a teacher you trust, a friend's parent, an older brother or sister, or another relative.

CHAPTER THREE

Alcohol

● QUIZ ●

WHAT DO YOU KNOW ABOUT DRINKING?

1 I can drink as much alcohol as I like, as long as I drink lots of water and eat as well.
True/False

2 Black coffee sobers you up.
True/False

3 Alcohol makes you feel happy and confident.
True/False

4 Four bottles of beer will affect a woman faster than a man.
True/False

5 Nearly everyone drinks.
True/False

ANSWERS

1 **FALSE.** Water can help to dilute alcohol and stop you getting drunk, and eating, before or while drinking, can slow down the absorption of alcohol by lining your stomach, but you will still need to watch what you drink, because it's the amount of alcohol you drink that puts you over the limit, regardless of what you drink it with.

2 **FALSE.** Caffeine will give you a kick to make you feel more alert and awake but it won't get rid of the alcohol in your body.

3 **FALSE.** Alcohol is a depressant – it only gives you a small kick and then you'll begin to feel down again.

4 **TRUE.** Men have a higher body water content than women because they have a greater body mass, so alcohol becomes more diluted in their bodies.

5 **TRUE.** 90% of the population use alcohol as part of their social life.

WHAT IS ALCOHOL?

A lcohol is a drink that is, for the most part, flavoured water. Scientifically, it is a liquid made from fermenting sugar and yeast – a process that turns the sugar into alcohol. This is then mixed with water and congeners (chemicals that determine the taste and look of the drink). An alcopop is a fizzy drink with alcohol added, such as alcoholic lemonade.

To help you control your drinking, alcoholic drinks are labelled with the percentage of alcohol contained within the bottle. This helps you compare strengths of different drinks so you can drink sensibly and not get completely drunk every time you drink. The alcohol content is dependent upon how much water is added to the drink, and can range from anywhere between 40% (Whisky), 5% (Alcoholic lemonade) and1% (Low alcohol beer and wine).

ALCOHOL AND THE LAW

• **Buying alcohol** – buying or attempting to buy alcohol under the age of 18 is not allowed by law. If you are aged between 14 and 17, you can be fined up to £1000 (for 10–13 year olds, the fine is £250) for trying to buy or drink alcohol on licensed premises. In 1992 over 250 under 18s were prosecuted for buying alcohol. It is illegal to sell alcohol to someone under the age of 18 and a shopkeeper or pub landlord selling alcohol to someone below this age is liable for prosecution. Your parents are also committing a criminal offence if they buy you a drink in a bar when you are under 18 (although over 16 year olds can be served beer or cider with a meal in restaurants).

• **Drinking alcohol** – at present it is an offence for an under 18–year–old to drink alcohol in a licensed bar. If you're under 14, you're not allowed in a bar during opening hours. Between the ages of 14 and 18, you're allowed in a bar, but not allowed to buy, be bought or drink alcohol there. However, it is not illegal for you to drink at home or at someone else's home if you're under 18. Recently a Home Office paper has recommended that police be given new powers to tackle underage drinking. The proposal gives the police power to seize alcohol from under 18's. Under these plans teenagers found with alcoholic drinks on the street would have to provide an address and failure to do so could result in a £500 fine. In the States, young people are not allowed to drink in bars until they are 21, and then they may still be asked for ID!

• **Visiting pubs or bars** – you are allowed in a bar or pub once you are over 14, although you can only be served a soft drink. Some pubs do have a special license which will allow children under 14 into the bar area, provided they are accompanied by an adult. However, under the age of 18, it is illegal for you to buy, be bought, or be served with alcohol in a pub or bar.

WHY DO PEOPLE DRINK?

"I'm quite shy and need it to get into the party spirit." Mel (14)

"I like the taste." Lee (14)

"Everyone does it. If I didn't everyone would think I was a real square." Kelly (14)

"My parents said drinking is better than drugs so at least I'm not doing something dangerous." Sue (14)

"My parents do it all the time and it's never done them any harm." Paul (14)

"I do it because I get bored." Sam (15)

"The first time I got drunk I was 12 – I did it because I wanted to see what it felt like." Linda (14)

"I drink so people will like me." Karen (13)

It would be silly to pretend there are no good points to drinking alcohol, after all, if there weren't, no–one would drink. The fact is, people do drink to relax, be sociable and have a good time and this is fine, as long as they drink sensibly. In fact, moderate drinking can actually be healthy, for example, a single glass of red wine a day is known to have benefits for heart patients. It's when you don't watch your alcohol intake that you end up losing control, taking silly risks and getting ill. Drinking heavily also leads to violent and nasty behaviour, vomiting and dangerous accidents.

Drinking is attractive

DRINK MYTHS

"It makes you happy." Lee (14)

"It helps you to feel better about yourself." Sue (14)

"It gives you more energy." Paul (14)

"People tell the truth when drunk." Yas (13)

"It can't do any real harm." April (13)

"It gives you courage." Paddy (14)

While it's true that alcohol makes you feel happy, confident and energetic – the stimulant effect (the 'up' feeling) has a short life span and will soon be replaced by a huge down. This is because alcohol is a depressant and will make you feel miserable. It also dulls parts of the brain, which leads to a loss of inhibitions and judgement, which in turn can cause other problems.

"I used to have a real reputation for getting drunk and doing silly things. I'd get off with boys I hardly knew, and say mean things to people who were meant to be my friends. Finally, I went too far and stripped off completely at a friend's party. I thought it was hysterical at the time, but the next day I was sick to the stomach about it. I didn't go out for ages after that."

Debs (15)

Contrary to popular belief, abusing alcohol (i.e. drinking to excess) can harm you, even in the short term. About one thousand under 15s are admitted to hospital with acute alcohol poisoning every year as a result of drinking too much. Often they need to have their stomachs pumped and end up in intensive care.

WHAT HAPPENS WHEN YOU'RE DRUNK

"Drinking is great. It makes you feel happy right away. It usually makes me forget my worries about school and helps me to feel confident. When I feel it wearing off, I drink some more because the feeling's so great. The best laughs I've had have been when me and my friends have been drinking. Mind you, the mornings after are terrible. Sometimes, I can't remember what I even did the night before."

Lee (14)

How drunk a person is depends on how much alcohol they have in their bloodstream. The more drinks you have, the greater your body will be affected. Your speech will become slurred, your vision will become blurred, your balance will be lost and you'll become clumsy and accident prone.

Heavy drinking can result in unconsciousness, even death. Vomiting while unconscious or in a heavy sleep can cause death by choking.

Part of the problem with alcohol is that, unlike most food and drink, it is absorbed directly into the blood from the stomach. This means it remains in the body until it is burnt up by the liver. This usually happens at the slow rate of one unit of alcohol per hour.

Alcohol is measured in units and one unit equals:

- Half a pint of average strength beer or cider
  or
- A small glass of wine
  or
- A standard measure of spirits
  or
- Quarter of a pint of alcoholic lemonade

It is recommended that women drink no more than 14 units a week and men 21 units. This is because women's bodies contain about 10% more fat than men's. With less water to dissolve the alcohol, women get drunker faster then men.

If you're under 18, how you react to alcohol will depend on your weight, height, and size. Even though doctors recommend sensible weekly limits of 14 units (21 for men) – these are **ADULT** limits. These benchmarks do not apply to under 18s, neither are they targets to drink up to.

If you're going to drink, be sensible, take into account your age and size and do it carefully. Above all, remember the following:

- Alcohol is very high in calories. If you drink a lot, you will gain weight.
- Alcohol dehydrates your skin, making it look dull and prone to spots.
- Drinking will also affect your judgement and impair your actions, making you say and do potentially embarrassing and dangerous things.
- Some drinks are absorbed quicker than others, so their effects occur more quickly. For instance, fizzy drinks like alcopops hit your blood stream faster. If you drink quickly, you'll consume far more than you realise.
- Drinking can irritate your stomach and cause pain and diarrhoea.

SERIOUS HEALTH RISKS

Never mix alcohol with other drugs – it can be fatal.

Alcohol is a poisonous substance, so having it frequently milling around your body will harm you. Alcohol increases the risk of developing certain diseases and research shows that excessive drinking can damage the following:

- Brain: heavy drinkers suffer brain shrinkage and the loss of brain cells.

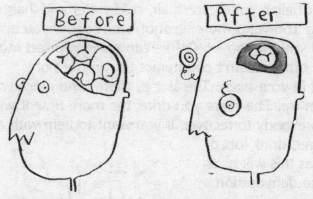

- Liver: if alcohol is present in the blood most of the time, it will prevent the liver from working properly, causing a disease called Cirrhosis which in turn can lead to liver cancer.
- Stomach: alcohol can cause serious stomach bleeding.
- Mind: alcohol is a factor in depression. It is estimated that alcohol is involved in about 65% of all suicide attempts.
- General health: vitamin deficiency, obesity and skin problems can result from excess drinking.

SOBERING UP

> "The worst thing about drinking is the next day. Hangovers are the worst. Headaches, being sick, feeling tired. It's awful." Charlie (14)

> "A good greasy breakfast with chips always helps." Sue (14)

> "Coffee and raw eggs are meant to help but I've never tried it." Tina (14)

A hangover is actually a sign that you've poisoned your body with alcohol, which is why you feel sick, have a headache and want to sleep. Contrary to popular belief, coffee, fresh air, cold water and 'hair of the dog' (drinking more alcohol) *won't* sober you up or stop your hangover. Coffee can make you feel more awake, but it doesn't counteract the amount of alcohol in your body. The fact is, there *is* no quick way to sober up. The more you drink the more time it will take your body to recover. If you want to help with a hangover, drink lots of water, as this will help with the dehydration that causes headaches and tiredness.

HAVE YOU GOT A PROBLEM?

"I don't need to drink but I do drink all the time, even if no-one else is. My parents don't say anything because they know I like it. Sometimes my mum will make a sarcastic comment but I just ignore her. It's my life, not hers."

Lee (14)

The first thing to consider with alcohol is how much you or your friends actually drink. Most people consider themselves to be sensible drinkers and yet drink way above their weekly unit allowance.

If you are worried about your habits, then start by putting together a drink diary for a month. Include every drink of alcohol you have, and try to note down where it was, how big the glass was and what you actually drank (be honest!). Then note how you felt the next day and how many hangovers you've had. This way you can see if you're way over the limit or drinking sensibly.

If you think your drinking is getting out of control, then you need to seek professional help, either through your GP or from one of the addresses at the end of this chapter. Warning signs to watch out for in others, or in yourself are:

- Being drunk more often than not.
- Skipping school because of a hangover.
- Having accidents because of drinking.
- Becoming touchy when people talk about drinking.
- Lying about how much they drink.
- Needing to have alcohol around.
- Drinking alone.
- Frequently mixing different types of drinks.
- Using drink to get through the day.
- Binge drinking on weekends.
- Becoming irritable and anxious if they can't have a drink.
- Not being able to make it through a night out without having a drink.

— Where am I? Who..

TIPS FOR CUTTING DOWN

- Drink slowly. The faster you drink, the greater the effect. Binge drinking is dangerous and people have died as a result of it. Remember it takes the average body approximately one hour to clear one unit of alcohol.

- Avoid drinking on an empty stomach; eating before you go out will slow down the rate at which alcohol enters the bloodstream.
- Pour your own drinks. This way you can keep track of how much you're drinking.
- If you're going to drink, then try to make every other drink a soft drink.
- Keep away from so–called friends who spike your drinks (add alcohol to your soft drinks when you're not looking) or try to make you drink more than you want to.
- Keep away from places where you know you'll reach for a drink, e.g. certain friends' houses, pubs that serve underage drinkers or off licences that will sell you alcohol.
- Don't be fooled by the new "soft" alcoholic drinks (alcopops). Many have an extremely high alcoholic content and because they are fizzy are likely to get you drunk quicker than you expect.

LIVING WITH SOMEONE WHO DRINKS

"My mother is an alcoholic. She pretends she doesn't have a problem but she drinks all day. By the time I get back from school she's either crashed out on the sofa or crying and saying she's sorry. When she's sober she promises to give up but she never does. "

Tom (14)

"My brother drinks so much. It's his friends really, they loaf about all day and do nothing. I often see them in the park getting drunk on the swings."

Annette (13)

"My dad is an alcoholic and I hate it. We're always having to cover for him when his work calls up. My mum pretends it's okay but I hear her yelling at him when she thinks we're all asleep."

Grace (14)

Many people drink alcohol as part of their social activities, however, if you know someone who turns to alcohol every time something goes wrong or uses it as a way to get through the day, then the chances are they have a problem. Before you start to try and help them, you need to help yourself – this means determining how badly their problem is affecting you and your life.

- If it's a parent who's drinking, ask yourself if their problem is putting your life or that of your sisters and brothers at risk?
- If it's a friend, boyfriend, girlfriend, brother or sister, are they a danger to themselves or to you when they drink?
  If the answer to either of these questions is yes, you need to seek outside help immediately.

It's hard to help someone who has developed a drink dependency, and sometimes the only way to help is to put yourself first. Even if you want to help them more than anything in the world, it's completely normal to hate them for what they are doing to themselves. If you feel disgusted or ashamed by their behaviour, don't take your anger out on yourself. Whatever your emotional state, you need to accept that their problem does affect you and that you will need help too.

Above all, it's important to realise that people who drink excessively do so to hide what's really scaring them. And sadly, until they admit they have a problem, they won't be able to overcome their dependence. In fact, no amount of begging from anyone they know will do them any good or convince them to change their ways.

HOW TO COPE

- Look after yourself and take steps to protect yourself, especially if you think you might be at risk.
- Don't blame yourself for their drinking. Each adult is responsible for him or herself.
- Don't pour away alcohol unless someone asks you to. Taking alcohol away from someone who is already drunk may put you at risk of being hurt.
- Don't cover up or make excuses to other people for their drinking.
- Don't be afraid to voice your concerns when they are sober.
- Tell another adult you trust what's going on. Share the burden.
- Contact Alateen and Al–Anon Family Groups. They are organisations which aim to help families of problem drinkers. Alateen deal specifically with teenagers who have been, or still are, affected by an alcoholic relative. The organisation is completely confidential.
  ALATEEN, 61 Great Dover Street, London SE1 4YF. Tel: 020 7403 0888.
  AL–ANON FAMILY GROUPS, 61 Great Dover Street, London SE1 4YF.

ALCOHOL – THE FACTS

- Alcohol is also one of the biggest killers in the UK. Twenty–eight thousand people die every year as a result of it.
- A third of young people aged between 13 and 15 have a drink once a week.
- 77% of girls have had alcohol by the time they are 13 years old.
- For 13 –16 year olds, alcopops are said to be the easiest alcoholic drink to obtain.
- 50% of 15 –16 year olds who drink every month buy alcohol for themselves.
- 51% of 15 –16 year olds drink alcopops.
- 25% of 13 –17 year olds get into fights after drinking.

FURTHER HELP

If you or someone you know has a drinking problem they need help with, your GP can refer you to local agencies who will help with detoxification (withdrawing from alcohol) and relevant counselling.

ALCOHOLICS ANONYMOUS, Head Office, PO Box 1, Stonebow House, Stonebow, York YO1 2NJ. Tel: 0904 644026.

ALCOHOL CONCERN, Waterbridge House, 32–36 Lonman Street, London SE1 0EE. Tel: 020 7928 7377.

THE HEALTH EDUCATION AUTHORITY have launched an interactive web site for teenagers and alcohol. Access the site at – **www.wrecked.co.uk**

DRINKLINE 0345 320202.

CHAPTER FOUR

Smoking

● QUIZ ●

WHAT DO YOU KNOW ABOUT SMOKING?

1 The majority of smokers want to give up.
True/False

2 A few drops of pure nicotine can kill you.
True/False

3 There are more young female smokers than young male smokers.
True/False

4 1-in-5 coronary heart deaths are caused by smoking.
True/ False

5 Most smokers start smoking between the ages of 12 and 18.
True/False

6 Inhaled smoke contains at least 4,000
different chemicals.
True/False

7 Low tar cigarettes are safer to smoke.
True/False

8 There are over 7000 smoking-related fires
each year.
True/False

9 More people die from smoking-related
diseases than through road accidents.
True/False

10 If you live with smokers, you're likely to inhale
secondary smoke equalling about 60-150
cigarettes a year.
True/False

ANSWERS

*Number 7 is false — there is no reduction in the
risk of having a smoking-related disease through
smoking low-tar cigarettes — but all the remaining
statements are true. They may seem excessive,
sensational, scary or downright ridiculous, but
the fact is they are all accurate comments on
smoking and very few people take any notice of
them.*

Most people know smoking kills. You only have to read the side of a packet of cigarettes to see how seriously dangerous they can be, and yet millions of people continue to smoke worldwide. Some do it because they are driven by a desire to participate in high risk activities, others do it because they're bored or want to appear something they're not. Many do it 'just because they do' and refuse to take the health risks seriously.

> "If they were really as bad as they're supposed to be, they wouldn't be on sale, would they? " Mark (13)

> "My mum's smoked for years and she's never ill." Donna (12)

> "I try to get my dad to give up but he says there are worse things he could do." Helen (14)

> "I like the taste and anyway it will be years and years before the effects start to show." Claire (14)

These are just some of the comments smokers give about smoking. Mark's comment in particular is a common one. After all, if smoking really is so dangerous, why are cigarettes on sale on the High Street?

Well, there are many reasons why smoking is legal, tax revenue being one of them. Cigarettes are, after all, big money for governments across the world. The UK government makes over £8 billion a year on tax from tobacco sales ($48 billion in the USA), £108 million of which is made from illegal cigarette sales to under 16 year olds.

There's also the question of logistics – although anti–smoking campaigners have been very successful, it would be pretty impossible to ban cigarettes completely, particularly in private and especially while they are still legal. Smoking is, however, under attack in the public arena, due to the dangers of passive smoking. Sports sponsorship by tobacco companies has now been outlawed and smoking in most workplaces, on many international flights and on public transport systems like the Underground is now banned. In big cities like New York, smoking is also banned in shops, restaurants and cafes, while in Arizona, USA, smoking is banned in *all* public places – including the street!

THE HISTORY OF SMOKING

Tobacco has been in Britain for centuries. It arrived way back in 1565 and for the first couple of decades its use was purely medicinal. However, by the 1600s it had become a social habit for rich men, who believed it was an aid to health.

But cigarettes didn't become big business until the late 19th century, when they became more widely available. By the 1920s women had begun to smoke too, as advertisers associated smoking with glamour and being slim. The Second World War built on this reputation by identifying cigarettes with patriotism, and soldiers were issued with cigarettes as part of their basic kit. Some tobacco companies even went as far as to suggest that smoking equalled competence and respectability.

Though health risks had been talked about since 1600 – when King James I published *Counterblaste to Tobacco* – they weren't taken seriously in the UK until 1962. This was when the first major report from the Royal College of Physicians produced clear evidence that smoking and lung cancer were related. The Royal College insisted that the government take action and in 1971 the first health warnings appeared on cigarette packages. Sales did drop for a while, but this only led advertisers to up their advertising and start pushing low tar cigarettes (which don't stop lung cancer) as an alternative.

THE LAW AND CIGARETTES

It is an offence to buy cigarettes below the age of 16. It is also an offence for a shopkeeper to sell cigarettes, cigars, loose tobacco or cigarette papers to anyone under 16, whether or not they are for their own use. While it is not an offence for an under 16 year old to smoke, or to be in possession of cigarettes, a police officer can confiscate cigarettes from any under 16 year old caught smoking in a public place.

WHY DO PEOPLE SMOKE?

Like drinking and drugs, people smoke for a variety of reasons: to cope with shyness, nervousness and social awkwardness, to appear sophisticated and to fit in.

"It helps you to keep weight off."   **Karen (13)**

"I'd like to give up but I'm afraid of getting fat if I do."
Becky (14)

Many women and girls say they smoke because it helps them keep their weight down or even lose weight. This is pretty much a myth. Studies show women who smoke are only marginally thinner (by about 1–2 lbs) than women who don't. Evidence also shows that very few women gain excessive amounts of weight when they stop smoking. In a recent study, only 6% of those who had stopped smoking said they had gained weight, while two thirds of ex–smokers said they felt better for giving up.

"It helps me relax." **Jules (14)**

"It gives me confidence." **Yasmin (12)**

Beliefs that smoking relieves stress, calms nerves and controls anger are all only half-truths. The fact is, smoking *does* have a slight narcotic effect – it makes you feel sleepy – but at the same time it has a strong stimulant effect as well – raising the body's blood sugar levels and promoting the production of adrenalin. In other words, it makes you feel more stressed out and anxious.

"It's cool." Tom (12)

"I'm just a social smoker. I only do it so I look attractive when I'm out."

Sue (14)

Thanks to advertising, smoking can come across as sexy or cool, but at the same time, it kills. What's sexy about that? It can also give you lung disease, heart disease and cancer. The fact is, it isn't easy just to have a couple of cigarettes now and then and resist them the rest of the time. The effects of tobacco are immediate and they continue to build up with each puff on a cigarette.

WHAT HAPPENS WHEN YOU SMOKE

When a person smokes, their heart speeds up, their blood pressure increases and they feel more alert. They become addicted to the nicotine in cigarettes very quickly and feel jittery, irritable and depressed if they aren't allowed to smoke. The smoke inhaled will then destroy their circulatory system, and coat their lungs with tar.

Without a doubt, smoking is incredibly dangerous. If you don't believe it, look at the following chart.

ACTION	RISK OF DEATH
Smoking	1 in 25
Motorbike accident	1 in 50
Car accident	1 in 600
Aircraft accident	1 in 10,000,000

(HEA 1980)

Lung Cancer

One third of all cancer deaths are caused by smoking. You are 24 times more likely to get lung cancer if you smoke more than ten cigarettes a day.

Chronic Bronchitis

This is a condition where the air passages to the lungs are narrowed and damaged and much of the lung tissue destroyed. By the time breathlessness occurs, most of the damage has already been done. Chronic bronchitis killed 30,000 people in 1992.

Skin, teeth and breath

Cigarette smoke smells and clings to your clothes, body and breath. You're more likely to have halitosis (bad breath) which can't be disguised with mouthwashes and gum and kissing a smoker is supposedly like kissing an ashtray. Nicotine in the cigarettes will stain your teeth and fingers yellow and your skin will become more prone to wrinkles, thanks to the chemicals you're breathing into your body.

Passive smoking

Breathing in other people's cigarette smoke can increase your risk of severe breathing problems and cancer. The smoke from a cigarette is divided into two kinds: Mainstream smoke, which is exhaled by smokers, and Sidestream smoke, which is released from a burning cigarette. This sidestream smoke contains ammonia, carbon monoxide and nicotine and is what makes passive smoking so dangerous.

HOW THIS EFFECTS YOU

- It is estimated that more than 1 billion cigarettes are consumed by 11 to 15 year olds each year at a cost of more than £120 million a year.
- Amongst 15 year olds it is estimated that 1 in 4 smoke regularly and 10% of both boys and girls aged 11 to 15 years are already regular smokers.
- According to a World Health Organisation Report, smoking will kill a million of these people world wide by the time they reach middle age.
  You may think these figures and health risks have very little to do with you. Maybe you've just started smoking or only have the odd one or two. Or perhaps you think that only long–term smokers like your parents will suffer from these problems. WRONG. Cancer cases are on the increase and smoking can only increase your risk of developing it. Try and give up – or better still, don't start!

GIVING UP

"I want to give up but I know it's practically impossible to."

Vici (13)

"I tried to give up once but it was too hard and all my friends were no help."   Stephen (14)

"I find girls who smoke a real turn off. My ex used to smoke and she wouldn't give up. She said if I loved her I'd put up with it. But I couldn't – kissing her was just awful."
                                                    Tim (14)

"I want my sister and mum to give up because they're killing themselves. I think if they won't think about themselves, they should at least think about me. I'm eleven years old. I want them to be around when I'm twenty."   Sarah (11)

Reasons To Give Up

"Boys like you better. My ex said he dumped me because I smelled of smoke all the time and it made his mum think he smoked."   Lisa (14)

"I gave up because it just got to hard to buy cigarettes and then when I did have them I'd always have to go out into the cold to smoke them because everywhere around here is non-smoking."   Angela (14)

"I'd give up if all my mates did because there'd be no point then."   Dee (13)

"My girlfriend asked me to stop because she said she hated it, so I did."   Paul (14)

"I wanted to be on the Hockey team but because I smoked I wasn't as fit as the other girls and so I didn't make it. My teacher suggested I gave up smoking for a while to prove to myself how much fitter I'd be. I tried it and she was right."
                                                    Sue (14)

Statistics show that six out of ten smokers would like to give up and hopefully all the above reasons will make you want to give up too. There are a number of ways you can stop smoking. Some people swear by going 'cold turkey', which means stopping completely straight away. Others need weaning off cigarettes over a period of time, with the help of nicotine patches and nicotine chewing gum, which help to hold off the cravings.

- If you want to stop smoking, the first thing to do is work out why and when you smoke. Stopping a habit isn't easy but with effort you can do it.
- Try not to say to everyone, This is my last cigarette for ever and ever – not only is this likely to tempt you back pretty soon but it will also get everyone badgering you.

- Take each day at a time and remember, just because you slip up and have one cigarette after you've given up doesn't mean you have to dive back in and smoke full-time. Don't give up, just keep trying.
- Don't put yourself in situations that will tempt you to smoke. This sometimes means changing your social habits or eating habits.

"I always had a cigarette in the park at lunchtimes. When I gave up I found I had to stop hanging out there because I was too tempted to have a puff."

Tom (14)

"We always sat in the smoking section in our local cafe whenever we went out. Now we try to sit as far away as possible. "

Tina (14)

Remember, giving up will result in an immediate improvement in health.

THE BENEFITS OF GIVING UP SMOKING

Within 20 minutes: Your blood pressure will fall.
Within 8 hours: Levels of poisonous carbon monoxide in your blood drop to normal.
Within 2 days: Your chance of a heart attack decreases and your sense of smell returns.
Within 3 days: You'll breathe more easily as your lung airways relax.
Within 2 months: Your lung function will improve.
Within 5–10 years: Your risk of lung cancer reduces to normal and premature wrinkling decreases.

TEN TIPS ON HOW TO GIVE UP

- Take one day at a time.
- Imagine all the money you'll save from not smoking. Try putting the equivalent money aside to buy yourself a 'reward' for giving up.
- Incorporate a get fit regime into your life. This will encourage you to keep away from cigarettes.
- Reward yourself for not smoking.
- Ask friends to support you, not nag you.
- Find ways of turning down cigarettes and practice them so you'll be prepared when someone offers you one. Just say no and don't offer any explanations as to why you've given up.

- Don't become an ex–smoker bore. No–one likes being lectured on their habits.
- Keep away from situations where you know you'll be tempted to smoke.
- If your parents or relatives smoke, suggest limiting smoking to one area of the house only.
- Question friends who won't respect your decision to give up.

TEN TIPS ON HOW TO HELP A PARENT OR FRIEND GIVE UP

- Don't lecture, instead talk through your worries about their smoking with them.
- Listen to why they feel they have to smoke. Some people can't see a way out and if you don't listen to their reasons why they smoke, you'll never be able to help them give up.
- Don't become their personal bodyguard. If they feel their every move is being watched, they may feel driven to smoke.
- Give them a break. If someone slips up and has a cigarette, don't bully them. Instead, encourage them to keep trying.
- If they are worried about putting on weight, try and get them to take up some kind of activity that will help them to cope with their anxiety. Swimming, yoga and keep fit are all good alternatives.
- Get them to change their habits. For instance, lots of adults smoke while having a cup of tea or coffee, or after a meal.
- Opt for non–smoking areas in cafes, restaurants, cinemas and waiting-rooms, this way there'll be no chance of having a cigarette.
- Emphasise the health benefits of not smoking.
- Keep complimenting them on how well they're doing. Mention improvements in their skin condition and breath, for example.
- If someone can't give up cigarettes completely, suggest cutting down initially.

SMOKING FACTS

- 450 children under the age of 14 take up smoking every day.
- A quarter of 15 year olds in the UK are regular smokers.
- On current UK patterns about 2 million of today's young people are going to be die from smoking–related illnesses.
- Teenagers smoke over £65 million worth of cigarettes a year.
- Smoking–related lung cancer in women has risen by 70% in under fifteen years.
- Smoking currently kills 3 million people a year worldwide.
- Income tax on cigarettes is over £8 billion in the UK, while Government expenditure on tobacco awareness is only £10 million.
- 61% of teenage smokers said they'd give up if the price of cigarettes was raised.
- When cigarette advertising was banned in Norway it halved the number of children who took up smoking.

FURTHER HELP

For tips on how to give up and more details contact:

ASH (Action on Smoking and Health)
109 Gloucester Place
London W1H 3PH   Tel: 020 7935 3519

QUIT (National Society of Non–Smokers)
102 Gloucester Place
London W1H 3DA   Tel: 0800 00 22 00 (helpline)

CHAPTER FIVE

Ecstasy

• QUIZ •

WHAT DO YOU KNOW ABOUT ECSTASY?

1 Ecstasy tablets are safe, as long as you know the person you're buying them from.
True/False

2 Ecstasy makes you feel calm and happy.
True/False

3 One Ecstasy tablet a week won't lead you to taking more.
True/False

4 Only people at raves take Ecstasy.
True/False

5 Drinking water counteracts the effects of Ecstasy.
True/False

ANSWERS

1 FALSE. People who sell drugs may tell you they know their tablets are pure but they don't. Most times, Ecstasy is mixed with other substances, such as Speed or glucose, and it's impossible to say what just by looking. Ecstasy is unlikely to be pure, as pure E is very expensive to produce. This is why it is normally mixed with other substances, to make it cheaper to produce.

2 FALSE. When Ecstasy has been mixed with another substance, you are less able to predict the effects and side-effects that will result from taking the drug. If, for example, an Ecstasy tablet contains LSD or Speed, your state of mind and where you take the drug will become an important factor in how the drug will affect you. If you're anxious and in a strange place you might end up having a bad experience with strong side-effects – such as panic attacks and paranoia – not happy and calm at all.

3 FALSE. Tolerance to Ecstasy develops very quickly. This means increasing amounts are needed to get the same high you originally got from only one tablet.

4 FALSE. Ecstasy has a reputation as a dance drug but lots of people take Ecstasy at parties and at home too, not necessarily at raves.

5 FALSE. Drinking water only stops you from becoming dehydrated. It doesn't stop the other effects of Ecstasy. There is also a serious risk from overdrinking. To avoid the effects of dehydration or excessive drinking of water, it's recommended that you drink at the rate of one pint of water an hour.

What do You know about Ecstasy?

WHAT IS ECSTASY?

> "Ecstasy helps you to relax and gives you energy to dance more." Tom (14)

> "Ecstasy is a love drug - it makes you feel happy and calm. When I take it, I always feel like going around and hugging people I don't know. It's brilliant." Tina (14)

> "The one time I took Ecstasy it was terrible. I couldn't stop sweating and had jaw ache from clenching my teeth all the time (something I couldn't stop). I also found I couldn't sleep. I just lay in bed, looking at the ceiling feeling knackered but awake." Paul (14)

Ecstasy – also known as "E", MDMA, XTC, Dennis the Menace, discoburgers, discobiscuits, lovedoves and M25s – is probably the most talked about drug in Britain. You can't open a newspaper without reading about its effects. If you believe everything you read, you'll no doubt think it's a one-way-ticket to death. What's more, you're probably wondering why so many people take it, if it's so dangerous. Well, the fact is, like most things that appear in the newspapers, reports on Ecstasy and what it can do for you (in a good sense and a bad sense) have been wildly exaggerated.

Basically, Ecstasy is a stimulant and an hallucinogenic drug that comes in a tablet form. It is a manufactured drug, known medically as MDMA (methylene-dioxymethylamphgamine). Most people think it's a brand new drug, but it was developed way back in 1914. No medical use was found for it until the 1970s when it was used in psychotherapy in America. By the mid 1980s it had become a popular drug on the US dance scene and soon made its way over to the UK.

Ecstasy was banned in the UK in 1977 and in America in 1985. It is a Class A drug, which means no doctor can prescribe it for you and anyone wanting to do studies on it has to obtain a special licence from the Home Office.

ECSTASY LOOKS LIKE: a white, brown, pink or yellow tablet or capsule.

WHAT ECSTASY DOES TO YOU

"E makes you feel as if you love everyone." Ian (14)

"It gives you loads of energy so you can just dance and dance." Sammi (14)

"At least it's not as dangerous as alcohol. When you take an E, the last thing you want to do is booze." Rob (14)

"It helps you to feel happy about your life." Will (13)

Dubbed the 'love drug' for effects that supposedly make you feel sexy, happy, affectionate or 'loved up', Ecstasy is said to make everyone feel peace and love towards one another. If this sounds too good to be true, you're right! In it's pure state, Ecstasy (MDMA) does do this, but these days it has become such big business that it's now impossible to buy pure Ecstasy without huge cost.

To keep prices down, tablets are mixed with everything from other drugs, such as LSD and Speed, to non–drug products like skimmed milk powder. This basically means it's a bit of a lottery as to which type of tablet you get and what type of effect it has. It has recently been estimated that less than 40% of the tablets sold as Ecstasy actually have MDMA present – which means you could be swallowing anything.

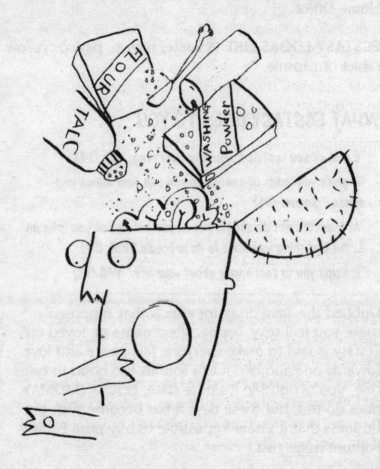

ECSTASY AND YOUR BODY

"How do I feel when I take E? Well, I feel like I've been given a huge shot of energy."

Carys (14)

"I feel like I could dance for hours and hours. I never get tired and just go around with this big smile on my face."

Carl (14)

Ecstasy (only if it's not mixed) is effective 20–60 minutes after swallowing. When it takes effect, your pupils will become dilated and your heart rate will increase. Some users may feel nauseous, hot and sweaty and their throat and mouth may feel dry (a sign of dehydration). You may experience an energy boost as your body's blood pressure and body temperature increase, which in turn leads to a feeling of euphoria or happiness.

This is the point when users report a relaxed, friendly feeling towards other people. This is because Ecstasy, like most drugs, lowers your inhibitions, making you more likely to do something you'll regret in the morning!

"I went to this club because I fancied this guy I knew went there. During the night I got talking to him, took some E, danced, and then took more E. It kind of gave me the courage to chat him up and before I knew it we were getting off with each other. I ended up having sex with him behind the club. The next day I was horrified. I don't do things like that – and I felt really ashamed, especially as everyone knew."

Sarah (16)

DANGERS

Ecstasy has a reputation as the most popular 'dance drug' around. This is because increased energy from the drug allows users to keep going for hours without feeling exhausted. Ecstasy stimulates the nervous system and energises the muscles, allowing users to keep dancing for hours.

This makes the heart beat faster, causing users to sweat and their kidneys to slow down. This is bad news for the body, as important fluids and minerals are lost. This is why users should drink regularly (fruit juice or water, never alcohol) to replenish lost fluids, and take time away from dancing to cool down.

Another downside is that once the symptoms wear off, tiredness and a heavy depression can take over.

Other pitfalls of this drug include exhaustion, teeth grinding, jaw clenching, anxiety attacks, depression and insomnia.

Grrrrrrrrrrr

ECSTASY AND DEATH

"I read about Leah Betts and I worry that will happen to my brother who takes E. I've tried to tell him that but he just laughs me off. He says he can handle it."

Ellie (11)

"I read that it isn't E that kills you but dehydration and stuff like that. Does this mean E is safe as long as you drink lots? Or is it still dangerous?"

Phil (11)

The death of 18 year old Leah Betts is probably the most publicised Ecstasy fatality. In 1996, Leah Betts fell into a coma at her 18th birthday party after swallowing an Ecstasy tablet. The tragedy of her death led to much media hysteria and a call for harder measures to be taken against dealers. Like many of the people who have died after taking the drug, Leah drank too much water in an effort to avoid heat exhaustion and suffered kidney failure as a result. Some people say it wasn't Ecstasy, therefore, which killed her. Though true, the fact remains, if she hadn't taken Ecstasy, she wouldn't have died from kidney failure.

Since then her mother and father have pushed hard for better drugs education in Britain. They believe the key to handling Ecstasy and its dangers is clear and honest drugs education.

Fatalities due to Ecstasy have been from dehydration (Ecstasy causes the body temperature to rise, by speeding up your heart rate. So when you dance maniacally for hours, pints of fluid are sweated out and a fatal heatstroke can follow if you don't replenish the water you sweat off). There have also been respiratory failures, heart failures and brain haemorrhages. While Ecstasy doesn't always cause death directly, it was a major factor in all the above cases. If they hadn't taken it, they'd still be alive. Don't be fooled by what you read. Ecstasy is a dangerous drug.

LONG-TERM USE

Ecstasy is not physically addictive but most of the worst side effects and experiences occur in those users who have taken Ecstasy regularly over a period of time, or use high doses, e.g taking more than one E in an evening (known as 'stacking'). These effects include psychosis, panic, confusion, hallucinations and loss of confidence.

There is also growing evidence that using Ecstasy for a long time may cause long-term depression. Research recently completed shows that the drug triggers mid–week blues after weekend use, in people who don't usually get depressed. The study showed that Ecstasy seriously affects the levels of serotonin in the body. Serotonin is the body's natural painkiller, and, while Ecstasy increases the levels of this within the body, the high is short–lived (like alcohol) and means the user will soon come crashing down to earth and be more prone to depression and sleep disorders.

HOW TO LOOK AFTER YOURSELF ON ECSTASY

If you take Ecstasy already, and have read the above section, you probably think you know how to look after yourself. Maybe reading about all the negative points hasn't put you off and you're still tempted to take it. If this is the case, there's not much I or anyone else can say. However, if you and your friends think you're adult enough to make a decision to take drugs, you should all be adult enough to make sure you can cope with it. Below are the things you should remember if you're going to take Ecstasy.

Chill out

It's vital to chill out when you take Ecstasy, even if you don't feel like it (and you probably won't). You might feel you could dance forever, but your body needs time to recuperate. Your heart needs to slow down and your body needs to cool down. Take breaks and make sure your friends do too. Be sensible, find a cool place where you can sit down, calm down and relax.

Don't dehydrate

Dehydration is the most important danger to watch out for because it can kill you. Dehydration occurs because Ecstasy makes the body's temperature rise, and continual dancing will make it rise even further. Because of this, you will sweat buckets. To replace lost fluids, users need to drink water at the rate of about one pint an hour and replace lost salts by taking something salty (fruit juice, fizzy drink, sports drink) as well. However, remember, don't overdrink as this is just as dangerous.

Don't drink alcohol

Alcohol and drugs never go together. As for alcohol and Ecstasy, this is probably the worst possible combination. Not only does alcohol also dehydrate your body, making you lose even more fluids, it will also react badly with other substances mixed in with the Ecstasy. If you want to drink, stick to plain water.

Look out for your friends

It's easy when you go out with friends to drive each other on to dance harder, party more and maybe even take more drugs. Maybe you've all made a decision to get totally off your heads. Perhaps you want a night to remember and are determined to get it. Whatever you decide, remember this – looking out for your friends is vital. Everyone responds differently to Ecstasy so even if you're having a great time, your friend may not be. Always make a pact to meet up at least once an hour and if someone doesn't turn up, make sure you go and look for them, after all, they may be in trouble and need your help.

Don't take too much

Stacking is a big problem with Ecstasy users. This is when you take an E, find it hasn't kicked in and take more and more, until you get the sensation you want. Stacking is a guaranteed route to an overdose because sooner or later all the drugs you've swallowed will kick in. When this occurs, your body will react violently, and you'll find yourself on the brink of disaster. Be sensible and patient. You don't need to swallow a huge amount of Ecstasy to get a reaction.

Take into account your size

All drugs work in relation to your body size. This means size, height and body weight play an important role in how strongly the drug affects you. If you're fairly lean and small, you can bet that Ecstasy will hit your bloodstream faster than an adult. Even if you don't have a small build, Ecstasy will still have a stronger effect on you than an adult. Don't be tempted to take large doses – if you have to try it, be sensible and take the smallest amount possible.

Never take Ecstasy on your own

This one is common sense. No drug should be taken when you're on your own for a number of reasons.

1 If you have a bad trip you'll have no–one around to calc you down.
2 If you get into trouble, there will be no–one to call for help.
3 If you pass out, there will be no–one to tell the doctors what you've taken (this is vital information for doctors who are trying to revive you).

WHAT TO DO IF A FRIEND BECOMES ILL

"The worst thing that ever happened to us was when my friend passed out on the way home from a party. We were at the bus stop when she started acting strangely, she said she felt sick and had pains in her stomach. I thought she was drunk because we'd all been drinking but then she just crashed out on the floor. I thought she was mucking about but she was out cold and breathing funny. It was horrible. I thought she was dead and started screaming. Thankfully, this man stopped his car and called an ambulance. On the way to the hospital her boyfriend admitted they'd taken Ecstasy. She was okay but she scared the life out of all of us."

Julie (14)

- The most important thing is not to panic. Warning signs of dehydration include not sweating, giddiness, cramps, vomiting, needing to pee and not being able to, and, of course, fainting. If you spot someone with these signs, seek help immediately.
- Whatever you do, don't give them any alcohol to drink as this will only dehydrate them further.
- If you're in a club or at a party take them outside, splash cold water on them to cool them down and make sure help is on the way.
- The best cure for dehydration is prevention. If a friend is insistent on trying Ecstasy then at least ensure that they drink water at a rate of about one pint an hour, are wearing cool clothes and take regular breaks from dancing.

- Heatstroke and dehydration can be fatal. If you see someone who has passed out, call an ambulance immediately. Keep them cool, loosen their clothes and don't leave them alone.

FURTHER HELP

NATIONAL DRUGS HELPLINE 0800 77 66 00
Manned 24 hours a day, this helpline is run by trained counsellors, available to anyone who has a question on drug or drug-related issues. It is friendly, confidential and sympathetic – and calls are totally free, so won't appear on your phone bill, unless you are on a mobile.

CHAPTER SIX

Solvents

● QUIZ ●

WHAT DO YOU KNOW ABOUT SOLVENTS?

1 People can die the first time they sniff glue.
True/False

2 It's not illegal to sniff glue.
True/False

3 Solvent abuse is most common in under 13s.
True/False

4 There is no such thing as a safe way to inhale solvents.
True/False

5 Gases and aerosols are more likely to kill you than any illegal drug.
True/False

ANSWERS

1 TRUE. *A quarter of all the solvent-related deaths are first time users. No matter how healthy and young you are, inhaling solvents can cause heart attacks and suffocation.*

2 TRUE. *Sniffing solvents isn't illegal because it's impossible to make solvents illegal.*

3 TRUE. *Statistics show that solvent abuse is more common in pre-teens.*

4 TRUE. *There is no way to safeguard yourself when you're inhaling.*

5 TRUE. *Inhaling solvents is deadly.*

WHAT ARE SOLVENTS?

Aerosols, glue, lighter fluid, paint stripper, petrol, nail polish, correction fluid, deodorants, anti-perspirants, butane gas, paint sprays, hair spray, fly killer, de-icers, household cleaning products, perfumes.

These products can be split into two groups: Solvents (glue, paint, nail varnish) and Propellant Gases which push out the product from the container (hairsprays, deodorants). All these products come under the general heading of Volatile Substances (that is, explosive or gaseous substances).

WHAT IS SOLVENT ABUSE?

Solvent abuse is most widely known as glue sniffing, but includes abuse of all volatile substances. Solvents give off intoxicating vapours or fumes which are inhaled in the search for a 'high'.

The number of ordinary household products that can be abused is huge, but, because of their widespread domestic use, it is impossible to make them illegal. The Intoxicating Substances Supply Act 1985 makes it an offence to supply a person under 18 with a substance which traders feel will be used for intoxication. However, as it is easy to assure people that the product is being bought for its original purpose only, this law is difficult to enforce.

HOW DO PEOPLE ABUSE SOLVENTS?

People who abuse solvents inhale the fumes and vapours given off by the above products. Substances like glue are often put into a plastic bag and inhaled through the nose and mouth. If an aerosol is used it is sometimes sprayed directly into the mouth, while fuels are often inhaled through rags. Hardly a sophisticated activity. What's more, the dangers of abusing solvents are huge (see below).

THE EFFECTS

"It's like being spaced-out and drunk. You feel light-headed, kind of out of it."

Fiona (12)

Inhaled solvent vapours reduce your oxygen intake which means your breathing and your heart rate are depressed (slowed down), causing disorientation, loss of control, visual hallucinations, headaches and dizziness. Some people have reported powerful delusions, such as thinking they can fly and pass through things. Like any hallucination, if you're caught in the middle of a bad one you won't be able to get out of it until the substance wears off. The key factor to these delusions and hallucinations is the user's mental state prior to taking the substance. This means that you need to take into account how you are feeling, where you are, what the atmosphere is like, who you're with and what you've eaten or drunk.

Users compare the feeling from inhaling solvents to be being drunk. But don't be fooled into thinking this is an easier route than drinking alcohol. Inhaling is very different and very dangerous. For a start the effects hit you much quicker because vapours go straight into your bloodstream (via your lungs rather than your stomach) and then directly to your brain. The effects also don't last long, sometimes only 45–60 minutes, which tempts users to try it again. And, if the effects of sniffing solvents is rather like getting drunk, the come-down can be compared to a very nasty hangover. You will feel terrible; tired, depressed and headachey.

WHY PEOPLE INHALE SOLVENTS

- **Pressure from friends** – Like all forms of drug abuse, peer pressure can play an important role in making people take up inhaling.

- **Boredom** – Believe it or not, this is a very common reason for taking up inhaling, along with depression and a desire for excitement.
- **Cheapness and accessibility** – For some people inhaling is appealing because solvents are low–priced and easy to get hold of.
- **Easy to carry about** – Unlike smoking, drinking or most other types of drugs, it's relatively easy to wander about with solvents in your bag. No–one's going to freak out if they see you with glue – and it's easier to explain away than Ecstasy. And there are no penalties for possession, because they are legal products.

"When I did it I'd forget all my worries. That's why I kept on doing it." Paul (12)

"It's easier and better than getting drunk." Marie (13)

"When I started it was just a laugh – a way of doing something wild without having to go and buy drugs." Carl (13)

"I get depressed so I do it. When I'm not doing it I get even more depressed so I have to do it some more." Allie (12)

"We all used to sniff, usually every day after school in the park. Then Jason and I started sniffing on our own at home. When I broke up with him, I stopped. I think now I only did it to be in with him." Suzanne (12)

"Sometimes I wonder why I do it. It's good for a little while, then I always feel miserable, tired and sick. Sometimes I even feel like killing myself." Tony (12)

"We were bored and didn't think any one of us was going to get hurt. I look at what we've done now and I can't believe we took it so far." Sam (13)

"I did it for a while, so did most of my friends but we gave it up pretty quick. You'd have to be an idiot not to." Andy (13)

"I started doing it in the bathroom when I was 11, after hearing someone talk about it at school. I'd just spend longer in the shower so no-one ever guessed at home. It was a way of coping with stuff. I hated school, and couldn't handle the other girls there. It seemed to help me get through the day. " Louise (16)

"I had big problems and felt I couldn't tell anyone. My mum and dad were getting a divorce and my sister had gone off to live with her boyfriend. I felt in a mess and couldn't talk to anyone. When a friend suggested I tried inhaling lighter fuel I thought – why not? I needed something to lift me." Gail (13)

"I was a glue sniffer for two years. It turned into a complete nightmare. I was so scared – I had these horrible visions where things were after me and wanted to kill me. You don't realise how it's screwing you up until you stop." Tom (15)

A lot of people inhale solvents to blot out other problems they're having in their lives, such as physical or sexual abuse. Others do it to be in with their friends or because they can't think of anything else to do. Sadly, as all the people above have realised, problems don't go away just because you sniff glue. Once the effects of the solvents wear off, the problem will still be there, plus an added problem of having to come 'down' off the high.

TELL-TALE SIGNS OF SOLVENT ABUSE

- Mood swings, from intense happiness to misery.
- Spots and sores around the mouth and nose.
- Acting as if they are drunk.
- Sniffing and red, runny eyes.
- Strange chemical-like smells, and weird stains on clothing.
- Acting defensive when asked.
- Sleep problems.
- Confusion, depression, and truancy.

— Are you OK?

THE DANGERS

- All aerosols contain three main elements: the actual product, a solvent to stop it becoming solid in the can and a pressurised liquid gas to push it out of the can. Sniffing this gas directly means you may inhale a variety of other chemicals, as well as the actual product, which may produce additional risks.

actual product

Cleaning fluids

paint

Liquid gas

Solvent

AEROSOLS

"Cough" = "croak"

- Aerosols and cleaning fluids sensitise the heart to excitement and effort, meaning that if users inhale and rush around afterwards the heart can fail.
- Inhalants tend to smother the part of the brain that restrains your behaviour, leading to a lack of concern or control. Effects are unpredictable, ranging from a loss of anxiety to aggression and a spaced-out feeling. People under the influence of solvents are more likely to do something silly, like crossing a road without looking or climbing on to a steep roof, which could lead to injury or even death.
- Another danger is developing a tolerance to these drugs. The body does eventually become used to the effects of solvents, so, in order to get the same high, users have to take larger and larger doses, increasing their health risks.

SOLVENTS AND DEATH

The most important danger of all with solvents and inhalants is the risk of sudden death, ranging from suffocation to poisoning:

- There is a chance that you may pass out and choke on your own vomit.
- Aerosols sprayed directly into the mouth can cause suffocation and heart failure as your airways freeze.
- Inhaling fumes from plastic bags may lead to suffocation.
- Sniffing lighter fuel can cause death through the toxic effects of the fuel.
- Repeatedly inhaling petrol leads to lead poisoning.

LONG-TERM USE

In the long-term, the variety of chemicals you inhale from these products will affect your heart, damage your lungs, liver and kidneys, and destroy your nervous system. Regular users end up with constant headaches, sores around their mouths and noses and may also suffer from convulsions, depression and weight loss. A person sniffing repeatedly will look pale and suffer from tiredness, forgetfulness and a loss of concentration. Regular solvent users can develop a physical dependence on them, with corresponding withdrawal symptoms when they try to give up.

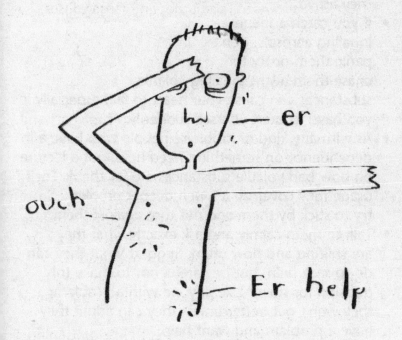

WHAT TO DO IF YOUR FRIEND IS INHALING SOLVENTS

- If someone collapses after inhaling drugs, check that they can breathe properly, turn them on their side (so they won't choke if they're sick) and seek urgent medical help. Be sure to keep any evidence of what they've inhaled (if you're not sure what, look out for an empty bottle, a paper bag, a tube, or an aerosol) and give it to the paramedics when they arrive.

- If you catch a friend inhaling aerosols, don't panic them or try to chase them away. Inhaling volatile substances can cause your heart to fail, especially if you have to exert yourself suddenly.

- As with any kind of problem, people who have a dependence on something need help, not a lecture on how bad volatile substances are for them. Their usage may cover up a much deeper problem. So, try to stick by them and not turn against them.

- Talk to them calmly and ask exactly what they are sniffing and how often. Suggest what they can do to seek help, but be careful not to make this decision for them. Like anyone with a problem, they won't get better unless they can admit they have a problem and want help.

- If they do decide to seek help, offer to go with them to see a GP, counsellor or drug agency. Above all, encourage them to believe that they can and will get over what's bothering them.

HOW TO HELP YOURSELF

If you're inhaling solvents, there are a number of things you should ask yourself:

- Why are you doing it?
- Is it worth the downs?
- Do you want to get help?
- Do you wish you'd never started?
- Are you inhaling solvents to cover up other problems?
- What are the personal risks to you?

If you want to give up but are afraid you can't, don't be. Hundreds of people give up inhaling every day. Experts say its effects are a bit like giving up smoking. This means the first few days are tough and you might feel cranky, tired and irritable. But after that, everything will improve very quickly.

Most people can't give up on their own, but are afraid to seek support. If you can't turn to your parents, an older brother or sister, relative or your GP, try contacting the National Drugs Hepline on 0800 776600. This is a 24-hour helpline run by trained counsellors, available to anyone who has a question on drug or drug-related issues.

CHAPTER SEVEN

Cannabis

● QUIZ ●

WHAT DO YOU KNOW ABOUT CANNABIS?

1 Cannabis is the most widely used illegal drug
  in the world.
  True/False

2 Smoking cannabis is more dangerous to your
  health than smoking cigarettes.
  True/False

3 Taking cannabis leads to heroin addiction.
  True/False

4 The police don't bother to arrest you for
  cannabis offences.
  True/False

5 No-one has ever died from cannabis.
  True/False.

ANSWERS

1 TRUE. It is estimated that 200 million people throughout the world use cannabis. Four million people in Britain have tried it and over 500,000 use it regularly.

2 TRUE. It is estimated that the risk associated with lung cancer and cannabis is eight times higher than that of smoking.

3 FALSE. This is a popular myth, but there is no evidence to suggest a link between cannabis and heroin. For instance, there are millions of people in Britain who have tried cannabis yet only thousands who are addicted to heroin.

4 FALSE. More than 40,000 people are fined, and cautioned each year for cannabis possession.

5 TRUE. But while no cannabis-linked death has ever been recorded it would be foolish to think any drug was 'safe'. Cannabis has its dangers just like any other kind of drug.

WHAT IS CANNABIS?

Also known as: marijuana, hash, pot, grass, resin, dope, ganja, spliff, joint, wacky baccy, blow, weed. Cannabis is the name given to all the by-products of a green bushy plant originally found in Asia but now grown all over the world. Cannabis resin is probably the most common form of the drug. This is a soft, brownish-black substance that is usually mixed with tobacco and rolled into a 'joint' (cigarette shape). You may see it being sold in small lumps wrapped in foil or cling film. Cannabis also comes in its dried leaf state (weed), or stalks of the plant are sold (grass). Cannabis oil is also sold as a drug. Hemp is a harmless by-product of the cannabis plant which is can be used as a material for clothing and other uses.

THE HISTORY OF CANNABIS

Like many other drugs, cannabis has been used for centuries. The Chinese used it in their medicinal applications, as did the Egyptians, and the Ancient Greeks used it as a cure for wind! The Romans made sailcloths and rope from hemp, which is how it first came to Britain. Cannabis became more widely used as part of the 1950s jazz scene and later became fashionable as part of hippy culture during the1960s. While cannabis still isn't as talked about as Ecstasy, heroin and cocaine, there's no doubting that it's the most used illegal drug in the UK.

THE MEDICINAL EFFECTS OF CANNABIS

"I don't understand it. In the paper I read about a man in America who was arrested for taking cannabis. He was 60 years old and said he did it because it helped his arthritis. My mum said cannabis is good for lots of illnesses. Is this true?"

Tanya (14)

In Victorian times, doctors prescribed cannabis for many illnesses including breathing complaints, muscle spasms and stomach diseases. However, over the years, cannabis has fallen out of favour. Since 1971, doctors wanting to test out the medicinal effects of cannabis have needed Home Office approval. This means most of the evidence on the medicinal advantages of cannabis are based on very small trials. However, it has been found to be useful in relieving pain from arthritis, improving the appetite in cancer and AIDS patients and controlling muscle spasms in multiple sclerosis sufferers. Cannabis is also said to have an effective medical use in the treatment of Asthma, PMT and Glaucoma.

SHOULD CANNABIS BE LEGALISED?

"If cannabis isn't harmful like other drugs, why don't they make it legal?"

Tom (14)

"Cannabis must be bad for you, otherwise it wouldn't be illegal."

Sarah (12)

Legalising cannabis is a very hotly debated issue. Some people believe it should be legalised while others believe that this would be a step towards encouraging drug abuse.

People in the 'legalise it' camp point out that cannabis is safer than some legal drugs like alcohol, and it is therefore ridiculous that it's still illegal. They argue that legalisation would mean that public money (in the form of police time) could be concentrated on stamping out more dangerous drugs, and that if cannabis were legalised, there would be more control over its use, as prices and quality could be controlled like they are in Holland, where cannabis has been legal since 1976. Although cannabis is legally on sale in coffee shops in Holland, these shops cannot sell to under 18s, aren't allowed to advertise their products and aren't allowed to keep any other kind of drug.

While it is no longer a crime to have 30g of cannabis for personal use, it is still illegal to produce and supply it. Research in Holland shows that there has been no increase in use since cannabis was decriminalised.

On the other side, the anti-cannabis lobby point out that cannabis *is* dangerous. They feel that making it legal would encourage people to become heavier users and especially influence young people who may never have thought of using it. Many also believe that saying cannabis is okay to use will lead people on to harder drugs i.e be used as a gateway drug.

WHAT ARE ITS EFFECTS?

"It makes me feel laid back." Jake (12)

"It gives you a nice feeling with no side effects." Paul (13)

"It makes me feel calm, especially when my mum's going on at me." Linda (14)

"I've tried it a couple of times and it did nothing." Sean (12)

"I only tried it once and it was disgusting. I felt dizzy and then got really sick." Julie (14)

"It makes me really giggly." Tina (13)

"Sometimes when I take it I see things really clearly and it's pretty cool." Seema (13)

Cannabis tends to make people feel more relaxed and confident. Some people claim it makes them more creative and thoughtful. Others claim it helps them calm down, while it has no effect at all on some people. Physically it lowers the blood pressure and is not addictive.

The effects of cannabis depend largely on how it is taken, although usually it's rolled into a cigarette (known as a joint or spliff) and smoked. Both resin and grass are also smoked in pipes, or through water in a bottle or other container (a bong). Sometimes it is eaten in the form of cookies or cake, to disguise the taste. When it is taken in food or drink (such as hash tea), users can't know for sure how much they've taken and may not feel the effects for 30 minutes. When cannabis is smoked, its effects can be felt within a few minutes.

As with other drugs, the effects of cannabis depend very much on what the user's state of mind is at the time, and what their expectations are. Most people (if they are honest) don't feel much at first, and then gradually get to know how it affects them. On the whole, cannabis relaxes people and heightens their sensory awareness (vision, hearing, taste, smell). This means some people will become more talkative, while others become simply 'laid back'.

THE DANGERS

The real danger with cannabis, apart from the fact that it is illegal, is the state of intoxication itself. A user cannot drive or co-ordinate safely while under its effects. Regular users are more likely to be sleepy, clumsy, and unable to perform to their best abilities, so the likelihood of accidents increases, which means they shouldn't do things like drive or cross roads by themselves. They will also be less able to concentrate. Feelings of hunger ('the munchies') are also common.

Because cannabis in food takes longer to get into the bloodstream, you can never be sure how much you are taking in or how strong the cannabis is, which means you could end up having a pretty terrible experience.

> "My friend's sister made these cakes and didn't tell me she'd put dope in them. I didn't know what was happening to me, I felt really sick and started panicking because my throat felt like it was closing up. Thankfully, it didn't last long."
>
> Sue (14)

> "The space cakes we ate were so strong. It was horrible really because the room started spinning, some of my friends were sick and I just felt awful."
>
> Richie (13)

Other dangers of cannabis include being extremely sick if the drug is too strong, and passing out if you start drinking alcohol with it. Paranoia is another common effect of smoking cannabis. Many users claim they feel quite the opposite of relaxed and have a sense of anxiety and restlessness when they smoke.

LONG-TERM/HEAVY USE

There is some evidence that long-term cannabis use causes lasting damage to mental functioning (concentration, memory) and may affect your mental health. In heavy regular users it causes physical dependence and causes people to become more apathetic and lethargic.

"Between the ages of 14 and 17 I smoked cannabis all the time. Every day I'd skin up (make a joint) and smoke some, usually on my own. It was my way of getting through the day. It was a bit like: hassle at school – smoke a joint, hassle at home – smoke a joint. I thought it was a way of dealing with hassle, but it was just a way to avoid everything. When I was stoned (high) it was like nothing could touch me, but then I started to see I was really losing it. I didn't want do anything with my mates any more, my girlfriend chucked me because she said I was boring to be around and I failed all my exams. At the time I thought – who cares anyway – but then one day I realised I used to care, so I stopped smoking."

Mark (18)

Smoking cannabis also causes a higher risk of respiratory disease, including lung cancer, than smoking. This is because of the way it is smoked. Cannabis smoke is inhaled deep into the lungs and held there for a bigger effect. It also has a higher concentration of nasties like tar and gases, which means you are eight times more prone to get lung cancer than a smoker.

IS YOUR FRIEND TAKING CANNABIS?

Points to watch out for:

- Lack of co–ordination
- Red eyes
- Fatigue and tiredness
- Lethargy and lack of motivation
- Bad concentration
- Memory loss
- Spaced-out behaviour
- Needing more money than usual
- Being unmotivated about something they used to love
- Cigarette papers and tobacco lying about
- A strange sweet thick smell in his or her room (Cannabis has a very distinctive smell)

FEELING UNDER PRESSURE

"I don't want to smoke dope, but I hate being the odd one out. My friends don't force me but they go off to a room to smoke and I get left out. Even when they're not smoking it's horrible, because they're always talking about how brilliant it is."

Gina (12)

"There's a boy who sells grass at our school. He's always coming up to us and saying we won't regret it if we try some."

Yvonne (13)

If you're going to be under any kind of pressure to take drugs, it's more than likely that drug will be cannabis. Cannabis has a fairly "cool" reputation, meaning people who take it often want their friends to take it too. It's also far more of a group drug than others, simply because a joint is passed around from person to person, making it embarrassing and hard to say no. However, saying no to cannabis is like saying no to any other kind of drug. If you don't want to take it – don't let anyone pressure you into it.

FOUR POPULAR CANNABIS MYTHS

- **It's good for you.** Friends may try to persuade you into taking cannabis by telling you about it's so called medicinal benefits. While cannabis does have some health links, they're still not proven and even if they were, they would be unlikely to benefit the average user.
- **Everyone does it.** Lots of people do use cannabis but there are still plenty who don't. It's a personal choice and you should ignore anyone who tries this argument with you.
- **It will help you to relax.** Cannabis does help some people relax, but if you're feeling anxious prior to taking it, it's likely to make you even more anxious and worried.

- **You can't get addicted.** Cannabis isn't addictive but many people do become psychologically dependent on it. Heavy users start to believe they can't get through their day without it, and panic when they haven't got any to take.

CHAPTER EIGHT

Drugs, drugs, and more drugs

● QUIZ ●

WHAT DO YOU KNOW ABOUT DRUGS?

1 Speed helps you lose weight.
   TRUE/FALSE

2 An LSD trip can last for up to 12 hours.
   TRUE/FALSE

3 Injecting drugs is highly dangerous in itself,
   whatever the actual drug used.
   TRUE/FALSE

4 Amphetamines calm you down and help you
   sleep.
   TRUE/FALSE

5 **Magic mushrooms are illegal.**
TRUE/FALSE

6 **Anabolic steroids make you more masculine.**
TRUE/FALSE

ANSWERS

1 **FALSE.** Although it's true that in the 1960s amphetamines (Speed) were commonly prescribed as a slimming aid because of their appetite suppressant qualities, nowadays it is known that the appetite is only postponed and that as soon as the effects wear off, a user will feel ravenously hungry. Speed is now rarely prescribed, because long-term use leads to high blood pressure, heart problems and the possibility of a stroke.

2 **TRUE.** The effects of a trip can last for up to 12 hours and once started, it cannot be stopped.

3 **TRUE.** Injecting drugs puts a user at risk from skin infections, sores, HIV and Hepatitis C.

4 **FALSE.** Amphetamines are taken to speed up the heart and give you more energy. They are stimulants which means they keep you awake, even when you become tired.

5 TRUE AND FALSE. Magic mushrooms can be legally picked and eaten in their raw state, but are illegal when dried, cooked or made into tea.

6 TRUE AND FALSE. Anabolic steroids contain the male hormone testosterone. Women who use them are likely to develop male characteristics such as chest and facial hair, baldness and a deeper voice. But in men the reverse seems to be true, with some developing breast tissue and suffering from shrinking testicles.

ANABOLIC STEROIDS

> "My brother works out and I worry about him because he takes steroids. He says all his mates do and there's nothing wrong with them, but aren't they illegal?"
>
> Paul (14)

> "I'm tempted to take steroids because I want a good body like the ones you see down at the gym. My friends tell me taking them gives you confidence without having to try too hard. People talk about the side-effects, but I reckon it's worth it."
>
> Nick (14)

Steroids are the most widely used drugs amongst athletes and body builders and are increasingly also being used as dance drugs, so that people can look good on the dance floor as well as at the gym or on the running track.

The Effects

'Anabolic' means 'building up' - and these drugs build up muscle and strength. Steroids contain the male sex hormone testosterone which regulates growth. They are usually swallowed as pills (sometimes injected) and can be detected through urine tests. Steroid use is illegal in competitive sports and sports people and athletes are tested rigorously for signs of use. This is because steroids give users an unfair advantage. They increase muscle size and weight, make people more aggressive and competitive, and enable them to perform at a better, stronger and longer level. This is why steroids are also known as performance enhancing drugs.

The Dangers

Many people don't think of steroids in the same way as illegal or 'hard' drugs. This is because people are generally unaware of the serious health risks involved. At the moment, possession of steroids is not illegal, unless you intend to supply them. But they soon will be – the government is looking at classing them as Class C drugs (see page 20). The majority of anabolic steroids are obtained from the black market. A large percentage of these are counterfeit, which means that, as with other drugs, there is no way of knowing the drugs' actual content or dosage.

Using steroids during adolescence is particularly dangerous. Young people who use steroids are often influenced by their peers (50% of students surveyed in Arkansas, USA were introduced to steroids by their friends) and may have a poor body image. Starting using steroids as a teenager can create a dependency on the drugs, with users feeling that they are inadequate without the help of steroids. Make sure you know the facts.

Steroids can muck up the adolescent body's balance. They contain the adult hormone testosterone, which, when present in the body through steroid use, confuses it. The body signals that the growth process has been completed, halting hormone production before your body is actually ready, causing bones to stop growing and stunting growth.

The other dangers of steroids are pretty severe.
Regular use leads to:

- cancer of the kidney, liver and prostate
- heart disease
- high blood pressure
- muscle spasms
- acne
- impotence
- sleeplessness

- severe headaches
- irritability, aggression and violent behaviour
- depression and mood swings
- anxiety and paranoia
- hormonal problems
  If you're female and taking steroids, you can develop male features such as excess body hair and a deeper voice. Males can end up with a reduced sex drive and the development of breast tissue.
- HIV and AIDS is also a risk with those who inject steroids as they are likely to share needles.

Some body-builders have begun to substitute insulin (used by diabetics) for steroids, as a cheaper way to build muscle. There are severe and immediate dangers with this which can include dizziness, disorientation, loss of consciousness, coma and, in extreme cases, death.

SPEED (Amphetamine)

> "I want to try speed. I've heard it gives you loads of
> energy and has no side-effects."
>
> Tom (12)

> "Lots of people I know take speed. They buy it round the
> corner from where I live and then share it. My boyfriend
> says it's a really fun drug to take."
>
> Louise (13)

> "My friend's sister said she took speed to lose weight. She
> lost about two stone really quickly."
>
> Lisa (13)

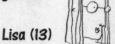

Also known as: Amphetamines, Whizz, sulphate, "A",
uppers, pep pills, diet pills, jelly beans, ice, crystal.
Speed looks like a white, greyish or pink powder.

The Effects

Speed is a stimulant. This means it wakes you up and
keeps you going. Once taken, your breathing and
heart rate will speed up and you'll feel energetic and,
sometimes, exhilarated. The effects of a single dose
last about three to four hours.

The Dangers

- Even at low doses, Speed can cause mood swings, temper tantrums, irritability and restlessness.
- Dehydration is also a problem, and users must drink a pint of water or fruit juice an hour to replace lost fluids.
- Taken regularly, Speed can produce mental confusion, panic and paranoia.
- Users also end up becoming physically run down because of lack of sleep and food, which leads to everything from bad skin to anxiety attacks.
- Heavy users also claim to develop an uncomfortable skin itching and severe depression.
- Like E, Speed is rarely pure. It's usually heavily diluted with everything from caffeine to baby milk

powder, aspirin, glucose and even ordinary flour! So users don't necessarily know what they are taking.

- Another problem with Speed is that tolerance to the drug rises quickly. This basically means more and more has to be taken to achieve the same effect. Regular high doses can lead to severe mental disorders which can take several months to recover from. Be warned.

- The effects of Speed can lead to a psychological dependence. Unlike a physical dependence which means the body literally craves a drug so that it can function properly, a psychological dependence means a person relies on a drug specifically to help them relax, escape or study. The prospect of being without that substance makes them extremely anxious and depressed.

- High doses and long-term use can lead to delusions, hallucinations and hostility, plus damaged blood vessels or heart failure.

COCAINE

"What's cocaine? I hear people talk about it all the time, but even though I know people who have taken E's, acid and smoked dope, I don't know anyone who takes cocaine."

Jules (12)

"My mum said she and her friends used to take cocaine when they were young and at parties and stuff. She says it makes you really moody and irritable."

Patrick (11)

"I hear cocaine is legal in South America. Is that true?"

Paul (12)

Cocaine usually comes in a white powder form and can be sniffed into the nose, or rubbed on to gums. It can also be smoked or injected. Crack is a smokeable form of cocaine. Cocaine comes from the leaves of the coca plant, which is grown in South America, where local people chew its leaves for energy. Cocaine is extremely expensive, which is why it has a reputation as the "in" drug for the rich and famous.

The Effects

The effects of cocaine last only 30 minutes, which means more and more has to be inhaled in order to keep the effects going. The drug works by being absorbed into the bloodstream through the thin membranes of the nose. The pupils become dilated and excitement levels rise. A user will initially feel cheerful and energetic.

Sniff

The Dangers

- Cocaine can quickly cause a large amount of anxiety, aggression and paranoia.
- Frequent use causes insomnia, depression and damage to the membranes of the nose.
- Repeated use has been known to produce disturbing and irrational fears and anxieties.
- Psychological dependence also occurs very quickly.

LSD/ACID

> "I quite fancy taking LSD. I've heard the trips you get are amazing. Colours, light, weird feelings – it sounds brilliant."
>
> Gill (14)

> "I took acid once and it was the worst. I felt sick and scared because everything went dark and frightening. The room looked like it was getting smaller and I kept imagining all my friends wanted to kill me."
>
> Sean (14)

Lysergic Acid Diethylamide (LSD) is an hallucinogenic, which means it has the ability to distort all your senses. LSD is actually a white powder but because only small amounts are needed for a trip, it is normally pressed into a small square of paper or gelatine. It is then swallowed and works in about 30 minutes.

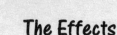

The Effects

Its effects are sensory hallucinations of distorted colour, sound and touch, otherwise known as trips. This might sound very exciting but taking LSD means risking having a bad trip as well as a good one.

The Dangers

- Having a bad trip – a bad trip is an hallucination that is frightening, depressing and scary – a trip from which you can't escape. Like most drugs, where you take it, how much you take and how you feel before you take it, all affect the sort of trip you have, for example, if you are anxious about taking acid, you are more likely to have a bad trip, as all your anxieties will be emphasised.
- Even a tiny amount of LSD can effect your brain. It could result in panic attacks or in some cases a permanent change of personality. Some users get flashbacks to trips, years after having taken LSD.

- Like all hallucinogenics, dangers arise when users try to do everyday things that require control, such as crossing a busy street or driving a car. Bad trips can also lead to unnecessarily dangerous activities, like jumping out of windows, thinking you can fly.

HEROIN

"If there's one drug that scares me, it's heroin. It's really dangerous and really addictive. My mum says all heroin addicts die so I must never ever go near it. But I still worry that I'll take it and end up a junkie. There are some people around here on it and they look terrible."

Wendy (13)

Heroin (or 'junk') can be taken by mouth but users often inject it straight into the bloodstream through a vein (mainlining) because it works more quickly. Once the most accessible veins break down through overuse (such as those in the arm), addicts will inject any part of their body in their desperate craving for a heroin hit, even going so far as to inject into the groin. Heroin can also be heated, and its vapours inhaled (this is known as 'chasing the dragon'). Heroin works by calming the user so that they feel nothing but a rush of happiness. However, when this wears off, users are left feeling numb. Unlike speed and ecstasy, heroin is a sedative, which means it slows down the body.

The Dangers

- Heroin is highly addictive. Though it is a common myth that one hit equals addiction, tolerance builds up quickly to all opiates (drugs derived from the opium poppy, including heroin), which means more and more of the drug has to be taken to have an equal effect.
- When not on the drug, users have severe withdrawal symptoms, including anxiety, cramps, fever, sweating and severe muscle spasms. This is called going 'cold turkey', and is often so hard to get through, that users go back to taking heroin, even when they no longer get any good effects from it, just so they can avoid having these withdrawal symptoms.
- Heroin addicts often neglect themselves and put themselves at risk due to the lifestyle they lead as addicts, for example, they often share needles when injecting, which can spread HIV between users.

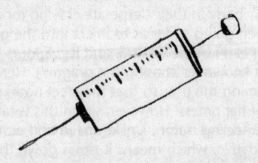

- Heroin users are more likely to resort to crime, stealing to support their expensive heroin habit, which can cost tens of thousands of pounds a year.

MORE HIDDEN DANGERS FROM DRUGS

Mixing drugs

Mixing drugs is bad news for a number of reasons. For a start it's practically impossible these days to know what's in a drug. Therefore, it's unlikely you can ever be prepared for all the effects, even when you know what you're swallowing. Mixing drugs is just asking for more trouble.

"I ended up in hospital the first time I took drugs because I did the most stupid thing. It was my 14th birthday and I went round to a friend's and got completely drunk on wine and cider. Then we took this E her brother had given her. After about 10 minutes nothing happened so I asked her if she had anything else, and she took out some Speed. That worked right away and then before I knew it the E had kicked in and for an hour everything seemed okay. Then I started to feel really sick and dizzy, and had this terrible headache so I went into her bathroom and took an aspirin. The next thing I knew, I was in hospital with a tube down my throat. It turns out I had passed out cold and been found lying in a pool of sick. It was terrible. I haven't touched a thing since."

Maria (18)

Taking drugs with people you don't know or like

All drugs alter your state of mind, which means you can have a good time or a bad time, depending on who you're with. If you're going to take drugs, doing it with people you trust is a plus for a number of reasons.

1 They'll look after you if something goes wrong.
2 They might be able to calm you down if you have a panic attack.
3 You won't feel threatened or scared by what they may or may not do.
4 They won't go off and leave you alone.

"I took acid once at a friend of a friend's house. I wasn't sure about doing it any way and kind of got pressurised into it. Once I'd swallowed it, I started to panic, not because of the drug, but because of what I thought was going to happen. A girl I didn't know started being really nasty to me, and saying I was a baby and should shut up. I felt terrible, I wanted to go home but knew I couldn't because of the acid, so I felt trapped. Of course, I had a bad trip and ended up screaming my head off."

Liz (17)

"I took acid with a group of so-called friends on a camping trip. Two of them knew I hated insects and for some reason they started teasing me about bugs and stuff. I ended up in tears and went back to my tent alone. I lay down and suddenly I started imagining that there were insects trying to crawl up my leg. I started shaking and screaming but they wouldn't go away. My friend (who hadn't taken any acid) said she had to sit with me all night because I was shaking with fear."

Tammy (16)

Drug-related crime

Drugs can lead to crime in more ways than one. In most cases it's a need for money to buy drugs that leads people to shoplift and steal.

"When I first started taking E, it was easy. My boyfriend ran a club, so I got E's off him. After a while he said I'd have to start paying for them because they were too expensive to just give away. I didn't mind because I only used to take one or two. But after a while I had to buy more than that, because I'd started clubbing all weekend instead of just Saturday nights. Also my boyfriend lost his job and I felt I had to repay the favour and get him stuff too. I went through all my savings in a few months, then panicked. I knew my parents would have a fit if they knew I'd spent all my money. I was only 15 and they had no idea how often I went clubbing. I always stayed the weekend with my older sister and she never told on me.

It was around this time that I started shoplifting. It started off with a few bits of make-up that I'd re-sell around school. Then it was clothes and CDs. A bigger problem was that though I was making money, I kept spending it on Ecstasy, so I never had any cash to make up my savings. I kept thinking I would stop. Every time I took E or took something from a shop, I'd swear this was my last time. Then I got caught. It turns out the shop had been watching me for weeks, so I couldn't lie and pretend I'd never done it before. I was 16 by then so I got charged, my parents found out, my friends found out and I got suspended from school. After that everything else came out as well. It was the worst time of my life."

Emma (18)

You may not be a drug user, you may not even be interested in experimenting with drugs, in fact, you may choose to keep away from them the whole of your life. Even if you do manage this (and lots of people do), you're still bound to come across people who don't share your views. They might be experimenters, or heavy users, or people who only do drugs on a social basis. Perhaps they'll be family members or friends, a boyfriend or a girlfriend. They might even be someone you work with or go to school with.

Their behaviour might worry you, or they may look like they need urgent help. Perhaps they're in some kind of trouble and looking to you for advice. This might scare you into keeping away or pretending it's not happening – drugs are, after all, a bewildering and frightening subject, and no–one would blame you for backing away. However, if you're ever confused or worried, you owe it to yourself to find out more. There are heaps of places you can turn to for confidential advice and information. All of the organisations below are there to help you. Don't be scared – ask for help.

USEFUL ADDRESSES

National Drugs Helpline – 0800 776600 (24 hours, freephone)
Alcohol Concern – 020 7928 7377
Al–Anon and Alateen – 020 7403 0888 (for families and friends of alcoholics)
Narcotics Anonymous – 020 7498 9005
ADFAM – 020 7928 8900 (for families and friends of drug users)
Release – 020 7603 8654 (24 hours)
Re–Solv – 01785 817885 (solvent abuse)
Crimestoppers – 0800 555 111

INDEX